Eye of the Storm

LEADING FROM PEACE WHEN ALL HELL IS BREAKING LOOSE

Brad Borkhuis, MBA

Copyright © 2016 by Brad Borkhuis, MBA.

All rights reserved. No part of this publication may be reproduced, distributed or transmitted in any form or by any means, including photocopying, recording, or other electronic or mechanical methods, without the prior written permission of the publisher, except in the case of brief quotations embodied in critical reviews and certain other noncommercial uses permitted by copyright law. For permission requests, write to the publisher, addressed "Attention: Permissions Coordinator," at the address below.

Brad Borkhuis - Founding Coach and Consultant
www.epitomecoachingandconsulting.com

Ordering Information:
Quantity sales – Special discounts are available on quantity purchases by corporations, associations, and others. For details, go to the website link above.

Eye of the Storm: Leading From Peace When All Hell Is Breaking Loose by Brad Borkhuis, MBA —1st ed.
ISBN 978-1-5371454-9-5

Contents

Why Is Leading Peace So Hard? 13

Do Right, Be Right, and Pay It Forward 23

#Attitude of Gratitude 29

Let Go and Have Faith 35

Peace Be with You 39

Know Thyself 43

Defining Your Principles and Philosophy 49

What Do You Value? 53

It's the Little Things 63

Internal Conflict Resolution 71

Define and Appreciate Your Support Network 79

Share Your Vision 83

Managing Up—Values as a Communications Tool 87

The WIIFM Principle 95

Creating a Peaceful Environment 99

Effective versus Efficient 105

Hire Slow, Fire Fast 109

Reward, Reward, Reward 117

Greatness Happens Every Day 121

So Simple, So Hard 125

About The Author

Tapped to be CEO at the age of 24, Brad Borkhuis found himself facing a $700,000 loss and the need to turn the family company around quickly. As a result, he knows what it means to operate under immense pressure. Guided by values, Brad's experience comes from being involved in every department through the turn around. By engaging employees through their values to buy into the vision of the company he lead his company to profitability in less than two years. The lessons you will learn in this book come from the lessons he learned while leading his own company and learning from his own mistakes.

Today Brad travels the world helping other entrepreneurs and leaders find their peace and maintain it while dealing with the storm that accompanies leadership. Through Business consulting, leadership coaching, and speaking Brad is living his purpose: to assist others in reaching their Epitome!

~ Dedication ~

I dedicate this book to my mother Mary and Late father Roger. They taught me so very much about business and growing up watching them work hard and integrate is in so much of the business blessed me with perspectives that have served me so very well.

I also want to thank the many employees, clients, and business associates that have taught me so much. It is their efforts and lessons that have made my professional goals possible and taught me what it truly meant to lead.

Finally, I want to thank all those who have helped me along this journey of life to truly be at peace and realize the ability I have to let go and get to where I need to be. Peaceful in the Eye of the Storm

Introduction

Anxiety, stress, anger, burnout, and fear: All of these emotions can arise when you are a leader facing the continuous flow of ups and downs, crisis upon crisis that you must handle day in and day out in your role. Imagine looking at all of that chaos with a feeling of complete and utter peace?

The challenges we take on as leaders are immense and consequential—they affect our lives and those of our employees and customers. At times our burdens seem too heavy to bear, larger than that of even legendary Atlas. If you are a leader who can relate to this, know that I have walked in your shoes and felt this same range of distressing feelings. I have been humbled; I have watched all of my work fall apart; I have been incredibly stressed and anxious. I'll share more of my story soon, but right now I am here to tell you that I have found another way and that is what I want to share with you. I wrote this book to help you navigate those troublesome feelings; to learn processes and tips for creating more structure, vision, and contentment in your life; and, most important, to discover how to lead from a place of peace. For me, peace is not a destination or a static location. I have found that "peace" is a verb. It is thinking, acting, believing, and dreaming in a manner consistent and in congruence with our values. It is how we lead with integrity.

This book isn't a marathon of words without action. It is a guide to take action and make these principles part of your everyday life.

Who Am I?

***

I felt like I was drowning. I was reaching up from the bottom of the well and as I grabbed the top brick, it crumbled. I reached again and the next one crumbled. This happened again and again. A few months before, I had agreed to return home and take over the family business. I came back in November and in December I discovered that our financial statements showed a $700,000 loss. I knew going in that the company was struggling, but in no way did I ever think it was that bad. To top it off, there was not much equity left in the business to leverage to get capital needed for a turnaround. I spent early mornings and long nights researching, begging, and praying—anything to figure out how we could turn this situation around.

And then when I looked up, I found that the answer was right in front of me. It was in the great employees who had built this business from literally the ground up. My father had laid one of the first bricks and many of the employees who had been there that first day we started the business were still around. In my quest to save my family's business, what I tapped into turned out to be a transformative lesson for myself—one that would shape the rest of my life. Yet just because I had found the answer in that moment did not mean I realized it!

I spent many years trying to control situations, people, and outcomes, thinking that were true success – Control of my destiny. But it was not until I empowered those around me by tapping into what was most important to them, the business, and myself and had faith in the process, that I found a modicum of true success. In the years that have passed since then, I have discovered that most of my proudest moments have come through my greatest trials and that these have given me opportunities to become the man I had always hoped I would be.

What you're going to learn?

***

As you approach this book, I would ask you to read it not with just an intellectual mind but a ready one. A common dilemma I teach my clients to deal with is called "Failure to Launch" (FTL). This happens when we have all these ideas and intentions, plans for moving forward and achieving greatness . . . but then nothing happens. We simply fail to go about doing the work. When reading this book, know that you do not need to respond by completely overhauling your way of doing business or going about life. However, be prepared to implement just one of the concepts in the book—but do it really, really well. You don't have to do it all at once. This book will still be here and you can come back time and time again to implement the other steps and suggestions. One process implemented is worth more than a million dreamt about.

In Chapter 1 we will acknowledge the reality that leading from a place of peace is hard, REALLY hard. An examination of the factors that make it so tough will set the stage for us to directly address those issues and develop the tools to find this place of coveted peace. In Chapter 2 you will see why philosophy is so crucial and the way in which my own personal philosophy helped me in creating a plan to find, and keep, my own peace.

One of the most powerful concepts in the book comes to us in Chapter 3, the Attitude of Gratitude. In my experience the path to peace starts here, once this concept is understood and implemented in your life you will begin to see instant and profound changes in your life. Chapter 4 is all about having faith in the process of seeking peace and the path you are on. It is not easy to keep the faith when all hell starts breaking loose but without it you almost never will make it through. Faith is self, the process, others, and a greater purpose is all needed to navigate the valleys and pitfalls of leadership.

Chapter 5 begins part 2 of the book where we focus on the tools you will need to be able to find, create, and keep the peace you seek. In this chapter we talk about the source of peace and the fact that it is an internal source, not external. It is here we discuss the concept of Loci of control. A fundamental concept to your peace is the ability to understand and apply this concept to a multitude of situations and results. We go into detail how to identify what we can control and what we can't and the importance of letting go, letting be, and loving in the life we have. Chapter 6 is a nod to Sun Tsu and his masterful work in the "Art of War". In his book he makes a profound statement; "If you know the enemy and know yourself, you need not fear the result of 100 battles. If you know yourself but not the enemy every victory gained you will also suffer a defeat. If you know neither the enemy nor yourself, you will succumb in every battle." In our lives we tend to spend a great time analyzing the enemy which may be an army or combatant or something as non-violent as a large book to read or another person with a difference of opinion. What we miss is we truly do not know ourselves to know whether we even want this victory, or to be right, or why we even care. We need to spend more time understanding us before we can truly lead from a place of OUR peace.

With Chapter 7 we start taking action! It is here that we build the foundation (or rebuild the foundation) upon which our peaceful, powerful, and prosperous lives. Keeping with the "P" theme we are going to define our Principles and Philosophy. You will see the power and essentialness of having a solid philosophy strengthened by active principles. It is the definition of this philosophy that allows us the clarity needed to tackle the landmark chapter of the book; Chapter 8 – What do you Value? It is here where we intentionally select the values that will guide our actions and habits that will be the functional activity that will bring us peace and allow us to maintain that peace while we lead… even in the middle of a storm! Just the act of intentionally defining your values will be significant and put you ahead of 95% of the rest of the world. To put you in the company to share the rarefied air of those who actually live it then we need to keep moving on to Chapter 9. In this chapter we take those values we identified in and we convert them to daily habits. It is in this physical action of actually LIVING our values that they root themselves at the cellular level. It makes not only your actions but even your REACTIONS and impulses of the subconscious to be in sync with the values you want to live.

In Chapter 10 we face possibly the most difficult reality we have to deal with for this book and possibly for your lives. We have bravely and proudly defined the values we want to live in our lives. Now we must take the painstaking effort or reaching into the dark corners of our world and lives and find the areas where we live a contradiction or we allow contradictions to exist. An example would be if we have the value of health but eat and drink unhealthy foods and drinks. Another might be if we have a value of respect and someone (co-worker, "friend", even spouse or parent) does not treat us with respect. Allowing either of these to exist in our lives will only cause misery. We must address them in a proactive manner. This chapter walks us through how to do that.

Part 3 of the book is where we take the values we have defined and live them in a way that they create an environment that fosters those values. Just as this whole process starts with an attitude of gratitude for what we have, Chapter 11 puts that gratitude into action. In this chapter we define and show our appreciation for those who allow us to be great! We take the steps of not just internally appreciating them but putting our words into action. Chapter 12 is where we take the outward action of sharing our vision for the organization and possibly world to all of those you lead and those who depend on you leading well. We go through not only the importance but how to do it well.

Managing and inspiring people are likely the most important and most challenging part of what you do. It is in Chapter 13 that we explore a concept I coined "Managing Up". It is in this chapter we begin to examine how do we get the most out of others and inspire them enough to be engaged in the process of making the vision you set for the organization a reality. All based on the values you have set forth. One of the more revolutionary concepts of the book is covered in Chapter 14. WIIFM (What's In It For Me) takes an age old frustration of leaders being asked this question and turns it on its head and finds the immense value in the question. It literally turns this negative concept into a positive one that you will ask them to ask again and again because it will make you and your organization better.

When I work with an organization I have only one non-negotiable portion of my contract. That is the statement that says: "I will lead by example" and is signed by the leader (Owner/CEO / Manager/ etc.) Chapter 15 is all about that creating of the environment we seek is our responsibility to lead that way, by our values. You will see where there are steps you need to take in your organization just like you did in addressing your personal internal value conflicts to support the creation of a peaceful environment. Chapter 16 encourages us to stay the course of the principles we know will be effective and not give for the quick and easy path of that which is just efficient. A major part of that is what we cover in chapter 17; Hire Slow Fire fast. Way too often we operate just the opposite of that because of our fears. Instead of quickly getting rid of a person (element) that our gut knows is not right for the organization we hold on for many reasons from hope to fear of who is going to do their jobs. Once we finally pull the trigger and lest someone go we hurriedly usher in the next person so we do not overload other employees or ourselves only to find out we missed a big red flag and the process begins all over again.

When we get good employees we want to keep them, so show it! Chapter 18 focuses on creating habits around showing your gratitude on a high frequency to make sure we communicate just how much we appreciate those we lead and work with trying to accomplish this vision we have created.

The final section: Practice your peace is only two chapters but it is where take that we have learned and make sure it is implemented daily, far into the future. In chapter 18 we look at how we do not have to look far to find greatness and peace in our lives. It is there every day in the smallest of actions which may seem insignificant but are enormous. In the final Chapter we recognize the "I get it" part reading a book like this. The concepts are very straight forward and may seem very common sense but the challenge comes in the commitment to living them every day and recognizing we will falter but what is truly asked of is to be able to have peace in the Eye of the Storm is not perfection but commitment to living our peaceful habits and striving for them every day, every opportunity.

I truly believe this book will bring you some clarity and guidance in how you can get through your own storm so you can lead others through theirs!

Part 1: Foundation

CHAPTER ONE

Why Is Leading Peace So Hard?

Is a leader the result of nature or nurture? Yes and yes. We cannot deny that some elements of leadership, charisma for example, come more naturally for some than others. To presume that these skills or gifts solely determine a good leader, however, is absurd. Becoming an effective leader requires a combination of hard work, self-reflection, confidence, humility, perseverance, and vision among other qualities. And surprisingly, a person's natural gifts can even be a hindrance in the development of these essential leadership traits. In this chapter, we'll talk about why it is so difficult to lead from a place of peace, from a place where your values align with your day-to-day actions and reactions to the challenges that you face as a leader. We'll also discuss the various roles an effective leader needs to take on as you manage business decisions and your team. If you are an experienced leader, this first chapter will resonate; if you are a new or aspiring leader, please know that the information in this chapter will help you be prepared to handle the challenges that await you and allow you to tackle them while staying true to yourself.

Although many people want to be leaders, few are willing to endure what it takes to become a good one. Some simply associate leadership with being "The Boss" or with the entitlements that go along with a position of power. If that is you, if you are not willing to bear the leadership burdens, please stop now. Just gently close this book and have a wonderful life. If, on the other hand, you are ready to do whatever it takes to become an effective and inspiring leader; if you are prepared to take the path few are willing to go down and even fewer make it through; if you are willing to be alone in the crowd, to work harder than everyone else, and endure being chastised for reaping more than others are willing to sow, then let us begin.

The Burden of Responsibility

It was 3 a.m., five hours after I went to bed. I had closed my eyes, but my heart refused to stop racing and pounding. It was one of those times where you can feel your heartbeat pulsating throughout your entire body, wondering if you're having a heart attack or if your heart may be getting ready to explode.

The night was silent, making my racing thoughts and pounding heart seem thunderous. This was happening because I was faced with making a decision in just three days that would have a substantial impact on our company and all of our employees. I had spoken with many about this and received plenty of advice, but the final decision was mine and mine alone. That is the burden of responsibility.

Ultimately, when you are a leader, your responsibility—and your biggest burden—is doing what is right for the organization. Without the organization, the entity that employs and serves everyone—there is no reason for you to lead. There is no reason for anyone to show up.

The burden can be enormous and it takes a great deal of inner strength, as well as support from others, to be able to succeed. But each time you do, you grow a little stronger, a little wiser.

Not only can the burden be immense, but it is also constant. When you take on a leadership role, you do not leave that responsibility at the office; you do not carry it only from Monday through Friday. It is with you at all times. The good news is that if you learn to own it, it will empower you. Though burdens can be a challenge, remember that without the burden of gravity your bones would never form; you literally would have no backbone.

The Various Roles of a Leader

Part of the challenge of being an effective leader stems from the fact that you need to excel in numerous roles. It's not enough to be good with numbers or to have a vision for growth or even to be an inspiring people-person. The burden of leadership requires that you become at least adept, and ideally skilled, at all of these roles and more. Here we'll look at just a few of the roles you'll need to take on.

Role of Counselor and Mediator

When you stop and break down how you spend your time and energy as a leader, it is amazing to see how much of yourself you devote to managing and addressing human emotional needs. That is one aspect of leadership that does not seem to be well addressed in business programs. Perhaps the topic is too complex and situational to cover, or perhaps it's omitted because it does not fit neatly into a course or book. Emotions and situations are extremely dynamic, so responses are difficult to chart and replicate. The best academic suggestion I can give here is to take as many psychology classes as possible. Aside from that, the school of hard knocks, listening, and experience will prove to be your best tools.

Remember, employees come from many different backgrounds and their perspectives may differ widely from your own—they will not always see the same image or problem that you do. It's always important, too, to remember that a great deal may going on in someone's life, developments about which you may be entirely unaware, that may prevent that person from truly seeing and correctly grasping your vision.

It is on these occasions that you must go into the role of a counselor. Many will say, "Leave your personal stuff at home," but if it relates to the person, does it not go where they do? Think about your own experience in that regard. It's not always possible to adhere to the categorizations we give our lives. You may really want to say, "Leave the drama out of the workplace," but for that to happen, you must give individuals a way to vent or channel those concerns in a way that is productive and that allows them to manage the pressure. By allowing this to just "be what is" and then focusing on a positive solution, we allow ourselves to gain a degree of peace from it.

Obviously, this stuff can get ugly. You may learn personal things about your employees that you never wanted to know, and afterward, you still have the burden of making sure it does not negatively affect the organization.

When my father was diagnosed with cancer, not only did it hit me personally like a ton of bricks, but since he was the patriarch of our company, I had to consider how our many employees would take the news. We knew we had to manage the information properly or it would shake the company completely apart. There is no training for situations like this; you only have your values, principles, and communication skills to help you through.

Even those employees who will become some of your greatest assets need counseling from time to time. Sometimes it is simple advice on protocol, and sometimes it relates to life issues that are personal and emotional. Again, there is no way to prepare for all of it; just listen, learn, and lean on your values to decide how to handle the problems and respond. You will be stronger, better, and more centered for it—and so will your team.

***

Conflict resolution is a skill I suggest you spend plenty of time developing. While you will hear me preach "conflict preparation," you will be faced with many obstacles of resolution, and how you handle them can be absolutely critical to the success of the person/ project/ team/ division/ organization. Yes, it is that integrated.

As most conflict stems from a confluence of misunderstanding and perception, your role of mediator is not one of picking sides, but rather one of guiding the parties involved (whether individual or group) in navigating the turbulent waters of disagreement to reach a final destination of peace and respect. Often, that will be hard. You will feel that this is a burden you do not want. But a resolution must be found, and so you must leverage your value, wisdom, leadership skills,you're your own peace to provide that solution. It's critical to know your values, trust them, and act consistently on them.

Role of Teacher and Coach

Whether blessed with skill, a good work ethic, or both, an individual's "talent" needs to be developed to achieve its full potential. Otherwise, it may be squandered and lost in frustration, creating a significant loss for both the individual and the organization.

Thus, the role of teacher/coach is one of the most important that you have as a leader. We all know that we are only as good as our team, but also that our team is only as good as the weakest link. In stressful times, we do not typically "rise to the occasion" but rather respond at our most solid level of training. The higher the level of solid or complete training the better the results.

In the teaching and coaching process, there are two major challenges—time and consistency. You must provide your "pupils" (your employees) with a consistent message that includes a vision point (goal) as well as correction markers to signal when they have drifted off course. And you need to devote enough time to this endeavor to ensure that your feedback is sufficient for them to clearly see your points and the markers you lay out. What's more, you need to do all of this while maintaining your existing workload and meeting your other commitments and deadlines.

You need to analyze and plan for this process before hiring new employees, and you need to make adjustments to it as you assess the current skill level of your new hire. In addition, you must ensure that this process is taught to and implemented by those leaders under your direction. And you must monitor developments to ensure proper feedback throughout the process.

Though it might seem ironic, one of the most important roles as a teacher and coach is that of pupil. That's right, pupil, student, padawan, karate kid to Mr. Miyagi.

To truly be a good teacher, you must always be a good learner. Always have a coach/teacher/mentor to whom you report in your life. Remember, you are never too wise or too old to benefit from some good advice and a different perspective.

One of the greatest gifts I was ever given in this area was when I served as a high school football coach. I started as a position coach and taught the technical "x's and o's" of the player positions. In this area the kids probably had very little to teach me, or so I thought. Then, when I was asked to be head coach, I realized that the role was about coaching as well as motivating the minds and hearts of the athletes. It was at this time that I understood all that my previous athletes had taught me about relating to them and connecting them to a purpose—and how little I knew about that before working with them. As a head coach, I opened up my ears and mind and learned so very much about personnel management, understanding alternate perspectives, and being at peace amid chaos. I am forever grateful for that experience.

Take some time right now to think about some of the skill teaching or mentoring you can do, and about the skill development or mentoring you need to receive to improve your life. You do not need to be the utmost expert in a field to help teach someone. If you are such an expert, consider what else you can learn to expand your mind. For this exercise, use the space provided or a separate piece of paper, and write down some people you can include in this circle of teaching and learning; then write out a plan for working with them. It is that simple, with a large added dose of follow through.

THOSE WHOM I CAN HELP:
1._____
2._____
3._____
4._____

EXPERT RESOURCES for my development:
1._____
2._____
3._____
4._____

PLAN OF ATTACK:
_____
_____
_____

Beacon of Hope

In your leadership role, there will be dark days and there will be turbulent waters. At times, you will question if there is a light—or a train roaring at you—at the end of the tunnel. When the worst happens, the many will look to the few for assurance that all will be okay and that you will get through this. Especially at these times, you need to remember one thing: You are a lighthouse, your employees' beacon of hope—whether you want to be or not. And bearing this burden does not relieve you from your own personal challenges. It doesn't mean you will not have trepidations or the same concerns that trouble the many.

Nonetheless, you must remember your post and serve as a guide through these rough waters.

As a beacon of hope, you must live by example and demonstrate how you want your employees to conduct themselves. Leading by example is by far the most powerful step you can take as a leader. I am not talking here only about how you conduct yourself in a meeting or at work, but how well you live a life of goodness in and out of the organization. Whether you are giving a press conference or spending some time completely alone, let your life be guided by, and in alignment with, your values.

In business and life, you must both be a beacon and have a beacon. I remember one time when I was really frustrated in business; we were taking two steps forward and three back, and the experience felt like this life-ending roller coaster. I was complaining to one of my mentors and then she started to share some of her experiences that sounded just as bad, if not worse, than mine. I asked her how they got through it. She said she always remembered the "Why." Ever since then I have had my own "why" and from that I defined my guiding vision. It is built of the following elements:

Purpose, philosophy, values, environment, goals, and relationships.

Knowing who you are, and who you want to be, in each of these areas and committing to them steadfastly (whether we are talking about you or your organization) is key to being able to lead from a place of peace.

It Can Be Lonely at the Top

The rarefied air at the top of any mountain, profession, or challenge is thin and makes it difficult to breathe. That is why many are afraid or do not wish to train and suffer to the degree that it takes to live at that "elevation," and for this reason it can be very difficult for others to relate to your issues.

In December of 2014, I was blessed with the opportunity to climb Mount Kilimanjaro. I trained for three long, grueling months. This included walking on a treadmill with an incline that matched the mountain, wearing a sixty-pound backpack, and restricting my oxygen for twelve hours a week through wearing a special mask. I also put in time stair-climbing and doing a cardio workout twice a week. It was rough.

When I talk about that training, people all get it; they understand. But when I go on and talk about air on the mountain—air so thin that you never really catch your breath, that your head and eyes hurt just from being there, where every step requires a conscious thought to move—they cannot relate. I tell a good story but there is just no context to understand that challenge. Others can understand stair-climbing and hiking while carrying weight, but the thin air is something they simply can't comprehend. That is what our problems as leaders are like. Unless you reach outside your organization to others in similar roles, you may find that nobody understands you.

To succeed as a leader long term, you will need to be comfortable with the fact that most people will be unable to relate to the challenges, issues, and struggles that constantly confront you. You will need to accept that nobody wants to hear complaints, especially from someone making more money than they do, so do not expect or seek such sympathies. To find support for yourself, you will need to go outside the organization and connect with other leaders or a mentor/coach.

Responsibility and accountability do not typically attract a crowd; they act like screening elements to ensure that only the qualified enter. This does not mean that the wannabes and "posers" cannot be given positions of leadership, but if you look at true leaders, they effortlessly accept the responsibility and accountability of the position but defer, or share, the credit.

"The Buck Stops Here"

A quote made popular by its placement on the desk of president Harry S. Truman, this phrase embodies the need for a true leader to stand up and understand that all blame and finger-pointing stops with you. No matter the problem, you must be part of the solution.

This phrase is one that must be with you at all times. If you want something to change or to be a certain way, you must lead by example. While the buck stops with you, it must also start with you. Leaders need to understand this: They will lead where to go by their own actions, their own example.

It's critical that you never pass the buck of leading by example and that you live a life full of habits congruent with your values. To be an effective leader, you must expect greatness from yourself every day and ask others to follow your lead. While this book offers the tools to lead with peace, it is up to you to implement them.

Follow the Beacon

When you craft a vision of the future and invest your passion and drive into it, you create a beacon for yourself and for others to follow through dark and rough times. This beacon is fundamental for strong leadership and must be built, shared, and constantly maintained. Without it, we and those we lead are susceptible to straying off course and even completely losing our way.

The development of this beacon is extremely important. It should be rooted in your values, principles, and beliefs. It is important to take the time to reflect and find within yourself what these are. This book is a good first step in that journey.

As a leader, you have a great deal on your plate, untold responsibilities to bear, and countless decisions to make. If you check in with this beacon when making those decisions, the resulting actions will support your greater vision. The higher the repetition of vision-based actions, the higher the likelihood that your vision will come to fruition— and that is something about which you and those you lead can get motivated.

CHAPTER TWO

Do Right, Be Right, and Pay It Forward

Defining "Right"

How we define words is essential in our communications. Without ensuring we are all communicating from a similar foundation and perspective, we run the risk of misinterpretation, and that can undermine the entire message.

To avoid that perilous misstep, let me tell you what I mean by "right." We all have engaged in discussions where both sides believed they were right. So how do we define who is more right? In the scale of right and wrong, there ranges from arbitrary (such as how words like "process" and "aluminum" are pronounced differently in American versus British English) to the moral (abortion, death penalty, stealing). For purposes of our discussion, "right" will be defined as follows: That sixth sense, gut feeling, premonition that tells you something is right or wrong. This is based on the values you have been raised with, combined with your ability to learn and assimilate new or correcting values into an inner voice that no matter what social actions, support, or resistance you receive, you just KNOW a decision or action is right. I call it "the right you can't lie to yourself about." Remember, this is about your actions, not judging others.

Now that we have established this common definition, which you won't find in a dictionary, the rest of the "Do Right, Be Right, and Pay It

Forward" concept will come together with ease. It took me a great deal of soul searching, analysis, and refinement to take all of my complex beliefs and perspectives and boil them down to a single philosophy.

How to Do Right, Be Right, Pay It Forward

Whenever I thought about my own personal values, goals, and relationships as they pertained to a difficult decision before me, I always heard echoes of my father saying, "If you don't find the time to do it right the first time, how will you find the time to do it twice?" As I revised my goals and reviewed what was important to me, a simple concept seemed to be at the cornerstone of everything. DO THE RIGHT THING!

Wow, so simple. Could it really be that simple? I started reviewing all of my goals and how I wanted to live my life through that lens. I began to truly listen to my "inner right" and followed it. As I did so, I noticed that difficult decisions and situations suddenly became much clearer. Granted, there are still situations in which I must sit and reflect and think, but as I began to listen closer to my internal compass, peace came over the decision-making and goal-setting process. I make this choice many times a day and, yes, I do make mistakes. When that happens, guess what I do? Yep, I do the right thing. The right thing is always in front of us, even if we make a slip up. Thus, the first part of my personal philosophy: Do Right.

When I interview Hall of Fame coach Dale Brown, the legend of LSU, for this book I asked him how he lived such an ethical life and he told me this story. "My Mother, two times in the middle of winter she had her coat on because she came back from shopping. Two times she asked me to go get her purse. One time she had $.40 and say the lady at the red owl gave me too much change and another time it was a quarter at the Piggly Wiggly, now with a mother like that how can you ever cheat?"

The next part of my philosophy, Be Right, came about as a way to evaluate and act congruently upon my environment, as well as my internal decisions and actions. Be Right refers to our responsibility to consider what we will allow to be acceptable around us. It is the macro to the micro Do Right focus, as well as the external versus the internal.

Here's an example: When you get a receipt back and notice that the cashier forgot to charge you for something, you go back and let the person know because it is the right thing to do. But what happens when the issue in question is at arm's length away and/or not a result of your actions? Your friend has the same experience at a store, but instead of going back in and paying for the item, he tells you how he got something for free. What do you do? The action is not forced upon you as doing wrong, but do you say something? Be Right means to give voice to the right thing that needs to be done or said and to affect your surroundings for good. Be a good citizen of humanity and this earth.

Finally, my favorite: Pay It Forward. This one will put your soul at peace; it will reward you more than anything else you can do. It takes love, consideration, strength, power, compassion, and so much more, and it does the most important thing you can ever do with those beliefs, emotions, or values. It turns them into actions. You'll find occasions to carry out this one many times every day once you start looking for opportunities. This is not a call to monetary support for all you meet (although there will be times where you feel compelled to give money, as that is the right thing to do). It can be as simple as a smile, a thank-you, a "I'm thinking about you," or any action that makes someone's day a little better. Trust me, not only will this feel good; it will also come back to you in waves when you least expect it.

Challenges You Will Face

Do Right, Be Right, and Pay It Forward rolls nicely off the tongue, doesn't it? If only living it was that easy.

The biggest challenge is that you must constantly make decisions. In some cases, it will be easy to make a good decision, such as when you are faced with a chance to steal. Other times, your options are a bit murkier, like more benign opportunities to tell a fib or to omit the full story. How many of these instances have occurred where an inkling of bad feeling arose, but we ignored it? The more you make good decisions on these smaller opportunities and temptations, the more habitual and second nature it will become to do the right thing by default. It is like the first month of a new eating lifestyle (notice I did not say diet!) or workout regimen.

The fact is that these challenging opportunities never leave you and you never become behaviorally perfect. The temptation to take the low and easy road will always be there, but after committing to making these good decisions and supporting this philosophy and lifestyle, you will feel lightness and contentment from taking this path. Further, I now notice that the dream is the reproduction of a little scene which transpired between my wife and myself when I was secretly courting her. The caressing under cover of the tablecloth was an answer to a wooer's passionate letter. In the dream, however, my wife is replaced by the unfamiliar E.L.

The Peace of Philosophy

When doing the right thing, fighting for the right things, and sharing your blessings becomes your default response, a peace emerges—the peace of having a good philosophy. Without a solid philosophy, you have no bedrock, no lighthouse to guide you through the storm of life. Take your time developing a personal philosophy; you do not want it to be something that's fickle and changes with the seasons or as a result of fads. Granted, experiences of life will greatly impact your philosophy and may alter or augment certain elements of it, but given time it should be robust enough to steer you through those times and remain steadfast.

The Foundation of Character

In the first part of this book, we will work on identifying the existing foundation of your character. This is a bit of a funnel-style assessment. You will be asked to look at the many influences you have had in your life (good and bad), your perspective on those influences, and how they have been the building blocks of your belief systems and thus, of your character. The reason I bring this up now is to prepare you to open your mind to ask questions of not just what you believe, but how and why you came to that conclusion and to ask, does it still apply? Some of these questions will be difficult and they may bring up strong emotions, but please do not put this book down and back away. By working through it, you will experience breakthroughs that will change your life and allow you to truly lead from peace.

CHAPTER THREE

#Attitude of Gratitude

Grateful Is a Perspective

Just like doing the right thing, being grateful is a belief and attitude that shapes our entire lives. The peace it brings is foundational, but this does not happen by magic. Being grateful takes the same dedication that you put into doing the right thing and it requires looking for the silver lining or gift within each event in your life. Sometimes this can be painfully hard, and often the reason for that pain does not reveal itself for many years, testing even the most patient person.

Take a moment to think about what it means to be grateful in different aspects of your life. Are you grateful when someone gives you a present? How about when someone steals your parking spot? Having a default perspective of gratefulness allows you to see that event in a different, unexpected way; instead of focusing on the wrong done to you, you will simply focus on being grateful for having a car that works well enough for you to find another spot. Perhaps you are thinking, "Much easier said than done." You would be right, but let's look at this from an analytical and logical point of view.

Think about something you are grateful for; really think about it and hold it in your mind—even close your eyes to focus on it. How do you feel? Did you smile a little? Now isn't that a wonderful way to spend the day, with that feeling running through your body? It comes down to a choice of focusing on the things that make us feel good, or the things that frustrate us, or the things flat out piss us off.

For me that is an easy choice, but it is still a choice. It is not being ignorant to the wrong done; it is putting the wrong into perspective within your life. I may address the wrongdoer, but I am going to do it from a place of respect and peace. After all, going back to the person who stole my parking spot, perhaps the driver did not even see me, or maybe her child is injured inside the building, or maybe some other troubling issue has diverted his thoughts away from the task of driving and being courteous. When you are intent on focusing on all the amazing, wonderful things in your life, the bad stuff that is bound to enter your world will not have near the bite. It's a matter of keeping things in perspective, that's all. Maintaining this attitude is a great way to go through life, but it does not come by snapping your fingers; it must be worked on like any worthwhile habit.

Here is one of my own examples that I call "Lessons of an Aging Friend."

I know the best size and brand of diaper to use as well as how to get the best fit for an aging basset hound. Now lord knows I would prefer to not need that knowledge in my life. I would rather be completely oblivious to the aging experiences of dogs, but that is not my reality.

Through the blessing of this lesson, I have gained a great deal of insight and empathy that serves me in everything from consulting, to basic listening practices. It also reminds me how much of the knowledge that serves us most in life comes from experiences we never want to have.

I was on a panel at my alma mater and a young person asked me what it takes to be a consultant, which many of the students wanted to be. I thought about it and then replied, "Many bloody knuckles." The audience chuckled a bit but I think they got it. The lessons I learned in the school of hard knocks were ones I had no interest in learning at the time, but looking back I am so grateful I did.

In life we will be given many opportunities to gain experience and knowledge in the midst of a situation that is tough, uncomfortable, scary, heartbreaking, and a litany of other words that describe NOT awesome.

Perhaps your reading this will give you an advantage I didn't have. Peace in the process, or at least an appreciation for the lessons you may learn.

Attitude of Gratitude as a Habit

Every morning I share with my coworkers at least three things I am grateful for every, single, day. It is my most important morning habit. Afterward, I listen as they share theirs with me. The things we are grateful for range from the materialistic to the spiritual, from serious to hilarious, and I look forward to hearing them and sharing them every morning.

Even though it is now a reactive habit, I still keep the reminder on my computer and phone that says "Time for Your Gratefuls" to make sure I do it. It is that important. If I am on vacation or climbing Mount Kilimanjaro, I still do it. It is that important. If I wake up angry at the world, I do it. Especially then, it is that important.

We all try to establish new, healthy habits. We start diets, workouts, plans for personal development; some of them fall off or fail miserably. The difference between the ones that stick and the ones that fail is the degree to which you make those decisions and actions important in your life.

Sharing Your Gratitude—Go Viral

As I mentioned, I share my gratitude every morning. I do this not to tell others about how great my life is, but to vocalize my gratitude and send it out into the universe. Try it; take something you are truly grateful for and say it out loud: I am truly grateful for _____. Then just sit in the reverberations and silence that follows. Cool huh? In addition, our sharing adds value to the lives of those who hear it; it may even remind them why they are thankful. Have you ever seen one of those Facebook videos or stories about someone who, in the face of huge challenges has overcome? An Amputee climbing Mt. Kilimanjaro, a homeless person so thankful for what they do have. The seeing of that brings instant humility and gratefulness to us. That's powerful.

This chapter starts out with a # and that is a nod to our ever growing social media culture. We see posts and videos go viral all the time: some disgusting, some sexual, some inspirational, some emotional. Look at your posts and walls. How do they look? You have a voice and your actions are part of that voice, so everything you post and share becomes your amplified voice to the world. Are you proud of what that voice is saying? Or is it saying nothing? Hash tags, posts, shares, and other social media activities can be part of you paying it forward. How are you making the social media world better? You do not have to be on Facebook or Twitter posting every day, and typically those people get ignored anyway. But if you are on social media in any form, pick your positive content and share your gratitude. Hopefully it goes viral. This world needs it.

Let's begin with a little practice. Below or on a separate sheet of paper, write three things for which you are grateful. It can be anyone, anything, any memory you want. Then pause to take a little time to think about them and just smile!

I am so grateful for . . .
1.
2.
3.

Great Things Happen to Grateful People

Have you ever gone shopping for a new car or phone or clothes and discovered there were more options than you had never noticed before? Most of those things had existed for some time, but YOU were the late one to the party. This same phenomenon occurs when we are practicing gratefulness. As you open yourself up to recognizing occasions, actions, or things for which you are grateful, you begin to recognize more options than ever. Then when someone asks you, "How's it going?" what you reflect upon are the great things in your life. Then when you respond, "It's going great, thanks," it's the truth. It is not just an automatic, glib response; it's based on your reality.

This does not mean your perspective of life will be all sunflowers and roses. Being grateful simply gives you a positive slant rather than a negative one. And you will find that to make a difference in yours and others' lives, it takes slants, edges, foots in doors, and tendencies that are incremental or slight, but that have profound effects.

CHAPTER FOUR

Let Go and Have Faith

This is one of the toughest chapters . . . ever. You have been raised and trained to press, challenge, take control, make it happen, be in charge, and now I am going to tell you that the path to peace is being sabotaged by many of those beliefs.

Let's first dispel this belief of control. In our organizations and life, we struggle to gain control, to be on top of all of the multitude of responsibilities and challenges that are presented to us. But what are we truly in control of? We think it is of our outcomes, but I am going to tell you we are so wrong. The most transcendent peace I ever found came when I accepted this. I do not mean to logically acknowledge that I cannot control everything. (Just like you may have responded when reading that statement.) I am referring to a true acceptance of that fact on our souls.

We are in control of very few things: our thoughts, our words, and our actions. That's it! Other than that, we can merely influence things. But often we mistake that influence for control. Take your car, for example. You control your actions of observation, the gas pedal, and steering, but you are not in complete control of the car. Think about a blown tire, engine problems, animal in the road, or even the road itself. You have no control over those things that can affect the outcome of the car or driving experience. This is the difference between internal and external locus of control.

Internal versus External Locus of Control

The difference here is important for you to not just understand, but to truly "get." This will allow you to have peace both when things are going great, and even when they most definitely are not. This is more than a perspective or thought—it's a belief and one that will take some faith to employ.

When we look at the self, there are elements that are, as stated above, under our control. They are our thoughts. This includes our perceptions, beliefs, and even dreams. They are our words, spoken, written, and implied. Finally, they are our actions—that which we do that affects the world, that allows us to influence and act upon our environment for good or for evil. Other than that, everything else belongs to the external locus of control that we do not have "control" over. Think about what that is and how much that is! It's basically EVERYTHING you see. Getting comfortable with this notion and not being scared to death by it is a difficult but necessary step in creating the headspace we need to focus on what is really important: creating peace.

Dale Brown had some great advice on this topic that came right from the great John Wooden. Dale said "One time I asked John wooden, my best friend, what is the one thing that made you a success. He said the one thing that stimulated me through life was as I was leaving to Purdue my dad told me. Johnny, Don't try and be better than anyone else but never cease to try and do your best and be the best you can be."

This is where your faith comes in. To navigate this new knowledge without faith will be paralyzing, but with faith you will enjoy a new freedom that allows you to have and find peace no matter the situation or chaos that swirls around you. I am not just talking about your spiritual faith but universial faith, which many times is grounded in your spiritual faith.

If your spiritual faith is strong, then when it comes to more earthly matters, we tend to be able to distance ourselves from the outcomes a little more. It's similar to what it's like to be playing black jack in a casino when you already have your original investment safe in your pocket and you are playing with the house's money. Although you don't want to lose, you are not as invested in the results of the game because of the safety and security of what you already have.

Universal faith is a true belief that doing the right things over and over again will lead to the right result, even if that result does not reflect the original plan. There is logic to support the premise that if we do all the right things we can in each situation, the best will happen. But it requires faith to stay steadfast to our beliefs when faced with the temptation of taking the proverbial low road or easy way out.

Let Go of Fear and Fear Not

It's like a master thief, one so efficient that you do not even know what is stolen, but one so insidious that it will steal that which is most precious to you. That is the skill and power of fear. The number of opportunities and situations that fear keeps us out of and puts us into is both alarming and sad.

Once upon a time, we may not have taken a chance, acted, or stood up because of fear. An opportunity or chance passed us by because we did not want to look "stupid." Or maybe we stayed in an unhealthy relationship for fear we would not find another, or we would not find something as good. Or we might have put on airs, avoided being authentic or honest for fear that we would look silly or not be respected. I know I allowed fear to affect me in all three of these ways. And as I look back, these incidents shaped my life considerably.

This is not about being scared; "scared" is a short-term acute reaction to potential negative outcomes. Once scared becomes a state, then it turns into fear.

I want you to know something important: YOU ARE NOT ALONE in this struggle. When you face these realities, I ask that you face them with humility and respect for the negative power of fear. (Kick fear's butt, but do respect it!) Fear leads to embarrassment, which leads to the crippling, horrible, never-right feeling of shame.

Shame is true, pure, unadulterated evil. It is fear's most dark, evil, nasty weapon. Shame is like the most powerful anaconda in the world slowly choking the life out of you. It is able to do this because it happens each time you make a decision to give fear power, and it happens so slowly over time as to be unrecognizable.

It is at work when you use words like "stupid," "lazy," "worthless," "not good enough," and so many other self-limiting or depracating terms. I ask that if you find yourself using these words, please stop and reflect on why you might be talking of yourself in this manner and address the challenges and fears that surround these words. Also consider whether they have progressed to shame—remember, you never deserve that. If you need to, gather the strength to reach out and ask for help.

If you're really believe that God is working through you the quality of your work will be so high that and you will receive so much inspiration every barrier will fall and you will be a blessing to all around you

In his famous poem, Dylan Thomas states: "Do not go gentle into that good night. . . . Rage, rage against the dying of the light."

I ask that you treat the night not as death, but as fear, and that you rage against it with your light and seek for good and for what is possible. Let's start with ourselves!

Part 2: The Internal Warrior

CHAPTER 5:

Peace Be with You

The Holistic Approach: Mind, Body, and Spirit

Like the traditional three-legged stool, you have a similar support structure. In the never-ending quest for balance, taking care of yourself and others requires that you address and readdress these three areas, as forces and events are constantly trying to pull you out of that balance. The holistic balance we all seek looks something like this:

Mind: You are stimulated and positively challenged in your daily thoughts and problem solving. You are mindful of the needs of your body and spirit, and work to allow thoughts that support you, not break you down.

Body: You treat your body as the only vehicle you will get to experience all of the dreams and visions your mind creates for your life. You respect what you put into your body, are conscious of what you do with your body, and you get proper rest. You listen to what your body is trying to tell you and you challenge, safely, your body for excellence and peace.

Spirit: You allow yourself to have faith, peace, hope, and wonderment. You listen to your inner voice and practice seeking and taking comfort in environments, internal and external, that create peace. You participate in activities that bring you joy and rejuvenate the soul.

How Well Have You Managed the "Asset" of You?

Many of us are always on the lookout for ways to improve our skills in leading others, whether through managing, coaching, teaching, supervising, or just being a friend. But right now we are going to start with the person in the mirror. When we do our initial assessment, we will examine ourselves in the three facets of mind, body, and spirit.

Many leaders make the egregious mistake of taking care of all of those around them—but not themselves—and then claim to be virtuous. This is dangerously misguided for one major reason: You cannot give from empty coffers. Remember you are the leader, and what others get from you is guidance, vision, strength, and shared energy. If you do not take care of yourself first, you will have nothing to share—you cannot give what you do not have. And if you do not take care of all three areas of yourself, you will eventually break down and your group will be leaderless.

Based on the above descriptions, let's take some time and do a self-assessment of how well you have managed these three areas of your life.

In regards to the following three areas I feel I am . . .

Mind:

_____

_____

_____

Body:

_____

_____

_____

Spirit:

_____

_____

_____

Finding Balance

It seems every day I find balance and then lose it a little. Balance — that coveted place of peace — is so tough to hold on to because it is always moving. Once you find it, there seems to be a million forces pulling at you, trying to drag you out of that peaceful position.

Maintenance Program

Any good program or undertaking requires maintenance to keep it performing at a high level. We are no different, and actually we tend to break down faster than many of the things we build—especially during the early days of our routines. This book outlines a process that will make your everyday maintenance routine worthwhile, as you begin to achieve higher rates of success.

Remember, the purpose of a maintenance program is not just to maintain the status quo. The real objective is to establish and maintain a rate of improvement. Consistently working on the skills and habits you will learn here, and being open to learning new things, is an important facet of being an effective leader.

As we discuss the need for maintenance and persistence, most will nod in agreement and logically recognize the need. So then why do we fail?

The Deadly Plateau: "I Feel Fine"

As you have made progress in various areas of your life, you have likely also had times when you reached a plateau and then, almost inexplicably, began to lose traction and progress, gradually sliding right back to that place from which you were trying to escape. We will help you make those changes part of your permanent life and turn "I feel fine" into "I feel great, and I don't want it to stop."

The inability to recognize suboptimum performance in our mind, body, or spirit is what leads to poor quality of life, disease, and, even, early death. We allow bad habits to build little by little and, before we know it, we are putting up with a burden of crap that is literally destroying our lives. Just as we would advise anyone else we see under a similar burden, we need to stand up straight and drop those bad habits. Drop that burden of crap.

Leading by Example

As this book states many times, if you want to lead, start by setting an example. It is by far the most efficient and effective way to give guidance on the actions, attitude, posture, or performance that you want to see in others. This is also a self-supportive activity consistent with the quote "If you want to really learn something, teach it." Teaching forces to repeat and reinforce the elements that are most important and worth passing along.

I cannot think of a leadership style or external power stronger than leading by example, leading the way and setting the bar of expectation by actually doing. We will dig into this even further later in the book, but right now I want you to make a commitment: As you read the concepts presented here, and see the value of their implementation and potential positive change in your organization, you will implement them in your own life first. Own the concepts, live them, then share them and teach them. Here we go.

CHAPTER 6:

Know Thyself

The Power of Your Beliefs

The last chapter offered an assessment of how well you have managed yourself in the areas of mind, body, and spirit. Now we will examine beliefs that relate to these areas. Belief, also known as "premise," forms our thoughts and our actions, which then determine our results. So understanding our premise is crucial to understanding why we are where we are. This understanding leads us to establishing the mind-set that enables us to overcome potential challenges which allows us to then achieve our vision.

Never underestimate the power of beliefs; the role of your premise in life is fundamental to the path your life will take. When we define your premises, we will do so in regards to the mind, body, and spirit, and it is important to understand and remember the power of these beliefs.

Identifying False or Limiting Beliefs

When people ask what our premises, or beliefs are, we usually think they want to know what our dreams are, or what our code for doing right is. We also must recognize that our limits are created by our beliefs.

When going through the process of identifying our beliefs, we must also identify what we see as our limits, and we must be able to understand and address them, so they eventually can be overcome. It does not serve you well to ignore your negative, false, and self-limiting beliefs and the power they have over you. Perhaps you are nodding in agreement but don't know how to go about identifying these beliefs. To get started, look at the limitations or negative views you have with regard to your mind, body, and spirit. Examples might be "I can never be in good shape," "I could never learn to do that," or any number of "I'm not good enough" that we tell ourselves. Once we identify these beliefs, however, we can analyze and address them. Never let a negative belief stop you from attempting something that you feel called to do.

Defining Your Premise

Now we can start the process of really getting to work and creating our position of peace. The first step is to define your premise. As you go through this process and the rest of the book, you will be able to tie that which is discussed on the last page right back to here. So let's begin by examining your premise, or what your beliefs are, in each of our three areas: mind, body, and spirit. You are simply going to take some time to reflect and answer the question of what you believe regarding the potential, limits, quality, and/or condition of your mind, body, and spirit. This book includes room for five statements, but you can add more if you'd like or use another sheet of paper.

When it comes to my mind, body, and spirit, I believe the following.

Mind:

Example: I believe I am good at figuring out math problems. (or I am not)

1. _____

_____

_____

2. _____

3. _____

4. _____

5. _____

Body:
Example: I believe my body is strong, and if treated well can overcome disease. (or the opposite)

1. _____

2. _____

3. _____

4. _____

5. _____

Spirit:
Example: My faith puts my soul at peace.

1. _____

2. _____

3. _____

4. _____

5. _____

Putting Your Premise to Work

Congratulations, you have just completed a task many have never even thought of doing; you have already created a clarity few can articulate. Now that you have taken the time to dig into asking the complex question "What do I believe?" you probably have a much clearer picture of how you got to where you are and what drives you.

But to ask the questions, tough or not, and stop there would be a huge waste of time! This is the rock upon which you will build your future. This tool that you created will make each of the next steps—in both your professional and personal life—a little easier and clearer, and in the end, more effective and peaceful. And that is why you are reading this book, right?

You will use this premise to give framework to your philosophy, and that will help you attract the positives in your life while clearly addressing the defined challenges. With that in mind, let's move on to creating your philosophy.

An example of how you will be able to use your knowledge of who you are and are not as Eric Joiner of AJC International. He stated about his skills "We were not good managers but we knew how to find really good people." By doing this they created a business that does over a billion dollars annually.

Defining Your Personal Philosophy

Everyone has a personal philosophy, and it is manifested in our actions. The problem is, that many do not have a consciously defined philosophy. So many of us go through life a slave to our impulses and short-term goals, slowly making our way through life on the path of least resistance. So, by defining your philosophy, you are giving intention to actions and to your life. We'll learn more about how to define your philosophy in the next chapter.

CHAPTER 7:

Defining Your Principles and Philosophy

To lead effectively, you must be confident in your principles, philosophy, and vision. This expands on the personal philosophy we talked about in chapter 6 and integrates the vision you have for both yourself and the people you lead.

Why You Need Principles, Philosophy, and Vision

In the last chapter, we defined a person's premise, or beliefs, as a sort of framework. Now we define principles as the steel used in the structure of the life you are creating. The stronger your principles (steel), the more resilient your life will be when you encounter inevitable challenges.

Defining your philosophy and vision opens the door to effective communication. With these elements in place, we can clarify how we are going to do what we are going to do, because we have a better understanding of what this means to us. The better you can communicate that to others, engage and excite them in the possibilities that you see and explain how you all can get there together, the better leader you will become. Never underestimate the power of good communication. If, in the end, it advances the cause and understanding, then it has the ability to create buy-in that would otherwise be unattainable. I always remind myself that a great idea poorly communicated is a bad idea. If the message is not clear and empowering, you will more than likely be very disappointed in the results.

A Principle-Based Philosophy

Again, principles provide the structure to your life, and your philosophy defines how you will approach the challenges, opportunities, and environment in front of you. We all see the need to do good in the world, but just how will we make a difference? Your philosophy is just that: a declaration of what you are going to do and how you are going to act.

Creating a philosophy guided by the strengths of your principles both opens your sails and is rigid enough to withstand the storms of life, even the storm of your own self-doubt. Creating a philosophy funnels all the work that you have done so far into a succinct phrase or feeling. Sometimes your philosophy is several pages long; sometimes it boils down to a few words. And sometimes it is an inexplicable sense of being that is compelling. As I discussed earlier in this book, for me, after years of thought, going back to the drawing table, and engaging in self-reflection and refinement, I have settled upon the following philosophy: Do Right, Be Right, and Pay It Forward. That short little phrase encapsulates my entire philosophy. It is a phrase, a thought—a philosophy—that guides my life day in and day out.

One of the best sources of philosophy I have ever found is Dr. Patrick Gentempo. When we talked about the importance of a good philosophy he had this to say: One of the best sources of business philosophy come from Ayn Rand. "Every business and human being has a philosophy; the only question is whether they know it or not. The reason it is so important is that if there are contradiction s in your basic philosophical premise or values the only possible outcome is destruction, and the amount of destruction is related to the amount of contradiction."

As I asked him what happens when someone does not have a strong philosophy. He gave me an epic answer. "Your values come from your philosophy, some people and business mindlessly adopt values or values become de-facto values the become part of the culture of a business without explicitly defining those value. If your values conflict with each other you end up creating confusion and confused minds do not buy and confused employees do not perform and confused owners do not make consistent decisions."

Now take some time for yourself and look back over your premise, values, and principles and establish a philosophy for yourself.

A Philosophy-Based Vision

As you can see, there is sort of a linear building process happening here, and that is on purpose. Effective leadership starts with yourself and then that framework gives you something you can replicate within others. But one thing that is difficult to replicate within others is vision. We can help and engage others to see our vision, but the creation of vision is a trait of a leader that sets them apart.

If I were to ask you what your vision is right now, I am guessing you could probably paint me a picture of fragments. A few people would be able to offer much more detail. Either way, through this process, we take those fragments and integrate them under the theme of your philosophy. If part of your vision is not congruent with your philosophy, then you are saying: "I see myself doing something that does not support my values, align with my principles, or support what I want to do in this life." When written like that, it seems a little preposterous, doesn't it?

Instead of thinking that you made a mistake or are confused, in some way, view this as a learning opportunity. Dig in and examine why you are holding on to that part of your vision. There are many possible reasons, some good and some not so good. But either way you must reconcile that disconnect. You may come to realize that this part of your vision is not what you want it to be, or you may need to go back and review your process of setting values to see if something was overlooked. Finally, you may decide to accept it as a known anomaly where it does not conflict with your values or philosophy, but I caution that this choice should be a last resort after a great deal of reflection.

When you have a vision that is supported by your values, principles, and philosophy, you create an extremely powerful, multi-focused system. When we are trying to develop our visions and we dream big enough, the path to get there may not be crystal clear, but we see landmarks and can sketch a general map. So you do not have to just stare at your vision and wonder, because every single action you take supports your values. Every time you stand for your principles, every day that you are living your philosophy, you are executing steps that will help make your vision a reality. You are now in control of your life's vision in so many conscious ways that your progress in each of these areas cannot help but lead to greatness. We'll talk more about creating and sharing your vision in chapter 12.

CHAPTER 8:

What Do You Value?

Great leaders embody a set of values and character. In this chapter, we will ask you to further define your values, examine them, and give them intention and power in your life, thus creating unshakable peace. One of the better value systems is the Golden Rule and as I found out in an interview with Dr. Bob Rakowski on the power of a good value system he said: "Value system keeps it level starts with having a deep caring for them, having an empathetic for where they are at but having with a coaching mindset to get them where they want to be to give them a hug when they need it and a kick in the pants when they need it because that is how I would want to be treated"

The Value of Values

Have you ever been told that what you are wearing looks dumb or doesn't match or is just "so yesterday"? Maybe someone said this to you bluntly, in so many words—perhaps it was a teenager or someone with weak social skills. Or maybe the person said it in a more veiled way, but that is the message you took in. Regardless, think about how you responded. What did you say? How did you feel? If you were young and impressionable, you probably felt embarrassed or crushed or, at a minimum, a little out of place. If you were an impressionable adult, you probably added being a little annoyed or angry to that list. I know that is how I used to respond to others' opinions before I found "My Style."

What exactly is that—my style? It doesn't have anything to do with my attire. Rather, it's about having confidence in my opinions and values, and respecting that others have their own opinions and perspectives. Simply put, it's knowing that I like what I like and respecting that. This does not mean that I am not reflective of my decisions or open to listening to other potential truths; it just means I respect myself and my journey.

The "value of values" is that they liberate you from others' opinions, creating a peace that helps you focus on what is important. When you are confident in your values, everything else falls to the periphery and become nothing more than distractions that you treat appropriately.

Have you ever been in a situation where you were asked to do something that you didn't mind doing, but you had another activity that you would really rather do? Let me give you an example. My niece asked me to attend one of her hockey games. At the same time a friend asked me to go to a concert of a band we had both long wanted to see. The game and the concert were the same day, but 700 miles apart; there was no way I could do both. I quickly and comfortably decided to go to the hockey game because not only do I value my family, but that specific event ranked higher than the value I placed on seeing the band. It ranked even higher than fellowship with that good friend. While I still love the band and my friend, my niece and her limited engagement game was just a higher priority.

You may think that supporting a niece over attending a concert sounds like an easy decision. You would be right; it was. But so is making the tougher decisions that come with being a leader. When you live by your values, most decisions become quite simple.

I had a client one time that had an option to get into a real estate deal. The deal would have been very lucrative and created some nice cash flow. They told me they decided not to pursue the opportunity. I knew some of the details of the opportunity so I was a little surprised to see them turn it down, so I asked, "Why? It seemed so positive." They proceeded to tell me that as they ran it through their filter of values the precarious nature of turning around this opportunity kept colliding with their value of joy. They would have made a lot of money but the amount of energy and time it would have taken away from their existing business would have stressed them both greatly, put both at risk, and taken away their joy they keep as a main value. Values may not make the decision easy but living them will make the answers very clear.

Where Do Our Values Come From?

If I asked you if you have values, I am certain you would say, "Yes, of course." But if I asked you to list your top seven values in order of importance or tell me where you have your top fifteen values written down, I am less sure you would be able to comply. So how, then, do you know you have values?

As with many of our habits, our values develop over time, beginning in early childhood. When I was young, I played a lot of sports. I was blessed to be successful in my athletic endeavors and I remember people asking me if my parents made me practice all the time or drove me hard. They didn't; I was pretty self-motivated. I do remember, however, one thing my parents insisted on: I was not allowed to quit a sport midseason. I had made a commitment, they said, and the team depended on me. That value of commitment was ingrained in me from my youth, and it has stuck with me to this day.

Values don't just appear out of nowhere. Indeed, some of our values evolve from lessons learned over years of hearing the same messages again and again from people we've grown to admire and trust. This includes parents, spiritual leaders, coaches, teachers, relatives, siblings, friends, TV characters, even books. As we absorb information into our psyche, both consciously and unconsciously, and integrate what we learn into our habits of thought and action, it's as if something clicks into place. And then—boom! Values are born, and they have the power to color everything we see and how we respond to what we see.

Without a doubt, we are influenced by the people who raise us, but what makes our values clear and present? It is something in our guts, what has become our sixth sense or moral compass. There is nothing wrong with having values passed down to us or sharing values with people we love and admire. But being a leader requires following our own moral compass and living in a deliberate way. It's time to ask: What if we gave conscious thought to our values and lived and chose our values with intention? What would happen then? What would we be like as human beings? What would we be like as leaders?

Defining Your Own Values

If I asked you to define California, each of you would probably offer a different definition because we all observe, analyze, categorize, and describe from our unique perspectives. This difference in how we define our environment also applies to how we define our values. We've just talked about how our values are influenced by the important people in our lives, but that's just one component of this definition. Our values are also shaped by the array of our own individual life experiences.

Defining your personal values is one of the most important intentional acts you can do in your life. Why? Because it creates power and ownership in your choices, direction, and in your life itself. Once we have defined our own values, the paradigm of rules and standards by which we live changes. Let me explain.

Have you ever crossed the street in an area outside the authorized crosswalk? Have you ever exceeded the speed limit? When you think about it, you probably acknowledge that those rules were created with good intentions and are designed to keep you safer, right? Now think about the last time you were chastised for "not following the rules." Maybe you weren't trying to be a rebel, but the rules just did not make sense or seemed silly to you. At issue is this: *You* did not choose the rules. When you choose to define your own values, however, you gain the power of ownership, empowerment, and choice over your values.

So, if you break one of the rules associated with those values, you know whose values you violated. Yep, your own.

Following is a list of values. As a first step in identifying your personal values, take some time to go through that list and put a check mark beside any values that resonate as being important to living the life you want by supporting your philosophy.

☐ Abundance	☐ Clarity	☐ Diligence	☐ Faith
☐ Acceptance	☐ Classy	☐ Diplomacy	☐ Fame
☐ Accomplishment	☐ Cleanliness	☐ Directness	☐ Fascination
☐ Achievement	☐ Comfort	☐ Discipline	☐ Fearlessness
☐ Acknowledgment	☐ Commitment	☐ Discretion	☐ Fidelity
☐ Affection	☐ Compassion	☐ Diversity	☐ Flexibility
☐ Ambition	☐ Competence	☐ Dreaming	☐ Focus
☐ Appreciation	☐ Completion	☐ Drive	☐ Fortitude
☐ Approachability	☐ Confidence	☐ Duty	☐ Frankness
☐ Assertiveness	☐ Connection	☐ Effectiveness	☐ Freedom
☐ Attentiveness	☐ Consciousness	☐ Efficiency	☐ Friendliness
☐ Availability	☐ Control	☐ Encouragement	☐ Frugality
☐ Balance	☐ Conviction	☐ Endurance	☐ Fun
☐ Beauty	☐ Cooperation	☐ Energy	☐ Generosity
☐ Belongingness	☐ Courage	☐ Enjoyment	☐ Genuineness
☐ Boldness	☐ Creativity	☐ Enlightenment	☐ Giving
☐ Bravery	☐ Credibility	☐ Entertainment	☐ Grace
☐ Brilliance	☐ Curiosity	☐ Excellence	☐ Gratefulness
☐ Calmness	☐ Decisiveness	☐ Excitement	☐ Gratitude
☐ Candor	☐ Deepness	☐ Experience	☐ Growth
☐ Care	☐ Dependability	☐ Expertise	☐ Happiness
☐ Certainty	☐ Desire	☐ Exploration	☐ Harmony
☐ Challenge	☐ Determination	☐ Extroversion	☐ Health
☐ Charity	☐ Devotion	☐ Facilitating	☐ Heart
☐ Cheerfulness	☐ Dignity	☐ Fairness	☐ Honesty

☐ Honor	☐ Mindfulness	☐ Prosperity	☐ Significance
☐ Hopefulness	☐ Moderation	☐ Prudence	☐ Silence
☐ Humility	☐ Modesty	☐ Punctuality	☐ Silliness
☐ Humor	☐ Motivation	☐ Quietness	☐ Simplicity
☐ Imagination	☐ Neatness	☐ Readiness	☐ Sincerity
☐ Impact	☐ Obedience	☐ Reason	☐ Skillfulness
☐ Independence	☐ Open-mindedness	☐ Recognition	☐ Solidarity
☐ Ingenuity	☐ Openness	☐ Reflection	☐ Solitude
☐ Inquisitiveness	☐ Optimism	☐ Relaxation	☐ Speed
☐ Insightfulness	☐ Order	☐ Reliability	☐ Spirit
☐ Inspiration	☐ Organization	☐ Resilience	☐ Spirituality
☐ Integrity	☐ Originality	☐ Resolve	☐ Stability
☐ Intelligence	☐ Passion	☐ Resourcefulness	☐ Stillness
☐ Intensity	☐ Peacefulness	☐ Respect	☐ Strength
☐ Intimacy	☐ Perfection	☐ Restraint	☐ Structure
☐ Introversion	☐ Perseverance	☐ Sacrifice	☐ Success
☐ Joy	☐ Persistence	☐ Satisfaction	☐ Support
☐ Kindness	☐ Philanthropy	☐ Security	☐ Supremacy
☐ Leadership	☐ Poise	☐ Self-control	☐ Sympathy
☐ Learning	☐ Popularity	☐ Selflessness	☐ Teamwork
☐ Logic	☐ Pragmatism	☐ Self-reliance	☐ Thankfulness
☐ Longevity	☐ Precision	☐ Sensitivity	☐ Thoughtfulness
☐ Love	☐ Proactivity	☐ Serenity	☐ Thrift
☐ Loyalty	☐ Professionalism	☐ Service	☐ Tidiness
☐ Mastery	☐ Proficiency	☐ Sharing	☐ Tradition

☐	Tranquility	☐	Uniqueness	☐	Victory	☐	Winning
☐	Trust	☐	Unity	☐	Virtue	☐	Wisdom
☐	Trustworthiness	☐	Usefulness	☐	Vision	☐	Wonder
☐	Truth	☐	Utility	☐	Wealth	☐	Worthiness
☐	Understanding	☐	Variety	☐	Willingness	☐	Zest

Focusing Your Value List

Nice job wading through that list. It was quite long, wasn't it? It is intended to be that way to help you explore more of yourself and to help you identify not only what resonates with you, but also what does not resonate with you. Perhaps you found stated values there that caused you to scrunch your nose and say, "No . . . that is not one of my values!" That's good; this helps you to better define the limits and topography of your values. In this section, we move on and work toward changing that topography from sand dunes to limestone. In fact, as you begin living those values, they will slowly evolve into granite.

So let's begin!

Quickly review the list above and all of the values that you checked. These values create a nebulous picture of what you would like your world to look like. While that's a good starting point, it is almost impossible to create specific actions from a list so large and diverse. So we are going to focus.

Go back to the list again, and now circle the fourteen most important values that align with your premise and philosophy. There will be a few values that immediately leap off of the page, but take your time to wrestle with the rest. We are not in a hurry for this exercise, so be thoughtful to ensure you are comfortable with your choices.

Take some time to do that now and when you are done, come back and we will continue.

***

Now you are getting more clarity about what values will create more direction, power, and peace in your life. Next we will take one final step of refinement and narrow that list down to the top seven. Carefully review the fourteen values you circled and put a big star by the seven that are most important to you. These will be your "actionable values."

Once you have ranked them in order of importance, list them below. It's okay if some are really close; just list them together and pick any order. Their ultimate order may become clearer to you as we go through the book.

My Top Values
1. _____
2. _____
3. _____
4. _____
5. _____
6. _____
7. _____

Why Are These Core Values So Important?

Like the North Star or a lighthouse, the values you just identified will be a guiding light as you traverse your path of life and leadership. As you face the ups and downs that will inevitably come your way, you will need something to keep you hopeful and humble and, most critical, something to ground you to what is most important in life. Values do just that, and our core values are the most efficient and effective tools we have. They will help you make decisions about issues large and small, and they'll infuse your life with deeper meaning and purpose.

Above, you were asked to select seven values for the seven days of the week—values never get a day off. Once these values become the "granite" we discussed earlier, you can look at living the other values you identified in this chapter. But I think you will find that by intentionally living this core seven, your other values will show themselves in big ways through your daily actions and habits.

CHAPTER 9:

It's the Little Things

Do the little things right and the big things will take care of themselves.

—Joe Paterno

This is one of my favorite quotes because it highlights the power in the little, seemingly insignificant tasks we do every day, every hour, every minute. In one of my Greatness Garage blog posts, I wrote about just that power of consistent habits.

Be Like a Latte

The other day I was making myself a latte at home. As I was steaming the milk, I was watching the thermometer that I stuck in the milk to know when I hit the optimum temperature. As I watched the needle, it seemed stuck at room temperature forever and then it finally started to rise. I noticed that as it got close to the higher temp, it seemed to take off and race toward the final temp. This was all as a result of a consistent heat applied over the couple minute period

> This made me reflect on how the consistent application of habits can have a massive and powerfully "quick" impact. In the early going, it is tough to keep the faith because it seems that our efforts have little to no results, but if we stick to it and keep the faith we can see the tide break. This is the power of consistency.
>
> We seem to see all the chips falling our way and are usually at a loss of words to explain why. We are grateful and sometimes use the word "lucky." Actually there is logic and even science working in our favor here.
>
> In the latte example, the heat causes molecules to move more and thus "bump" into more molecules, which bump into more and so on. In the focus of our goals, each positive action not only moves us toward our goal a little; it also gains support and aligns others around the consistency because they begin to see the vision more clearly and they get excited, much like the milk molecules.
>
> A client once asked me what is the best things they could do to attract the best employees and I said, "From a thirty-thousand-foot view, it is passion and consistency. Consistently living your values with huge passion has a power to attract those engaged with similar motivations."
>
> So keep on, have faith, live those values, and know that there is a storm of "good luck" brewing.

It seems simple, doesn't it? Little by little, step by step, all the great results come from doing the little things. It can't be this easy, can it? Yes! . . . and no.

Aristotle said, "We are what we repeatedly do. Excellence, then, is not an act, but a habit." Aristotle's quote succinctly describes why habits are so important.

Principle-Based Habits

In chapter 7, we focused on ways for you to discover the principles by which you live. Now, let's think about the habits that you create in light of those principles. If your habits do not align with your principles, then your principles do not align with your values. Ultimately then, that means your habits are not in alignment with your values, which leads to this unavoidable statement: My actions are not in alignment with my values, and without alignment between my values and actions, I will never find happiness, only misery.

"Don't just talk the talk; walk the walk." That statement, trite and worn as it is, very much applies to this concept because anybody can talk about values and sound like they are highly principled and believe in doing the right thing. But it is a much different thing to act in accordance with that belief. When we are deciding what habits we would like to create, we need to look at our philosophy, principles, and values and determine what actions will positively influence the strength, the existence, and the personification of those elements that represent who we want to be.

We sometimes define true greatness in the form of our goals, in our values, in our principles. But we live true greatness in our habits and actions. We must never forget that distinction—that if we do not live our greatness, then defining our greatness means very little.

Taking one step at a time can take you down the wrong path just as well as the right one, and any steps taken without the desired destination in mind is risky and has the chance of leading you toward negativity and ruin.

In this book, I constantly refer to and guide via the power of habits. Habits are the best way to conciously create a subconcious way of living or being. Habits also have the power to create legacies and to change lives forever. I used to weigh 325 pounds and I now come in at just over

230 and am much more fit. There is no diet or surgery or potion that has been the magic to my weight loss and keeping it off. It has been something I like to call "simple but hard."

From the simple side, all I had to do was choose to start buildiing little healthy habits, things that I would do over and over again. . . . BUT that is hard to do, especially at first. Over time, after making thousands of small good decisions, or creating habits, to support my value of being healthy, I saw the results much like the latte milk heating up. In the beginning, I chose to eat three very healthy meals a day and run at least one mile two times a week. It was tough to make that a priority, but what I found was that as I made it a priority, other good choices came more naturally and were less outside my normal habits or, as commonly said, they were "easier."

I kept this up month after month, year after year. I am now four years past that moment when I made a choice to live a healthy life intentionally and habitually. During that time, I have done a Tough Mudder obstacle race, competed in several triathlons, climbed Mount Kilimanjaro, biked a 150-mile challenge, done the insanity videos, the list goes on. I also eat fish at least three times a week, cook at least 90 percent of my meals, and read all ingredients (suprisingly, this is a big one for a healthy life).

Do I "sluff off" sometimes? Sure! Do I ever indulge in sweets? YOOOUUU betcha! But as a matter of habit, I support the value of a healthy life with my actions and I am able to reap the rewards of each positive choice I make.

While those good decisions helped give me a much healthier life, I have also struggled with many destructive habits over my lifetime. Overeating, speeding, correcting others, trying to control situations, being condescending, the list goes on. Think about a habit you have that does not benefit yourself or others or contribute to a healthy, peaceful life. What is one thing you could do, over and over again, that would curb the flow of that habit and possibly turn it back? Notice in my effort to create healthier habits and a healthier lifestyle, I did not create rules or restrictions like "STOP eating junk" or "STOP being lazy." That is because success comes by focusing on the positive actions we can take. Plus, a list of positives are easier to support and face every day than a list of No's.

Sometimes habits are easier to support in theory than practice. When we begin working to apply them, we struggle—in part because the challenge looks so big and in part because we are only trying to develop the habit that we are "supposed to" have, not that we want to have. Check out this Greatness Garage post I wrote on the subject.

How Do You Eat an Elephant?

As the saying goes, "How do you eat an elephant? One bite at a time."

It is used to reflect the need to see insurmountably large tasks in the manageable parts that make them up. I used this quote to set the groundwork for us looking at our own progress in life.

So many times we look at our progress in relation to an ultimate goal and often become discouraged, sometimes to the point where we cease to even chase our goal, and that is sad. In Expecting Greatness we talk about "managing up," the practice of focusing on the positive actions you can take to move forward or "up."

In this same way, I challenge you to look at the many goals you may have. Examine your personal, professional, physical, spiritual, mental, and other goals. Take comfort in where you are at—it is a great place to start—and decide for each what your next positive step is.

The focusing on taking the next positive step toward your goal is worth far more than wishing you could change the past. The challenge is the reality, consistency, and commitment. We need to make sure that the next steps are attainable; we focus on the consistency of the steps and obviously the commitment to the end goal.

The issue that most commonly arises is that we are not truly committed to the end result. It would be nice but it does not move us. On this you must be sure, and the other two steps will be much more attainable.

Have faith in yourself and your journey and remember, one bite at a time!

I Am My Habits: Time for Accountability

Once we recognize that we are our habits that we are the result of our actions, and then we can understand that our habits define who we want to be. When we dream, we understand that every dream must be followed by our waking up and taking action, by practicing the habits that we work to implement that day and the next and the day after that. This is accountability. Now, there are several ways to create accountability. You can ask others to help you out. You can have accountability groups. You can write it on the wall for the world to see to help hold you accountable. You can use social media, sharing it so others will help hold you accountable.

In the end, however, the most powerful accountability is and always will be self-accountability—that which is within you. If you are to succeed here, you must make living your habits an unalterable priority. That is the fundamental source of success. Your commitment to being accountable to yourself to do the little things is what makes true success and true peace possible.

But accountability often seems to have a negative connotation. Too often, it seems to be connected to placing blame or other negative deflections of responsibility. Accountability is really the ability to be accountable. The question is this: Do you have the strength to stand up, to represent your own life, and to say, "This is why I'm here, this is what I want to accomplish, and this is what I'm committed to do with a very high level of integrity"? Without that integrity, you can say whatever you want. The integrity ties your word to your actions. Your actions then become your word. And your word commands respect.

Stone by Stone

Greatness is built by our habits, and habits are built by repetition—by doing little things over and over and over again. Nobody builds a wall all at once. They set stones. But, stone after stone, the wall is created, guided by the values of strength and the vision of how the wall should look and function. In this same way, we build our character. We build the image that the world sees of us. We build the person whom we are. At the end of our lives when we look back, we will appreciate or regret not the goals that we had, but the stones that we turned or didn't overturn. It's the little things we do, whether in our personal or professional lives, that give value and create a difference in our lives and in the lives of others.

Habits are a tough thing to create because they take time. It seems that anything, especially in today's society, that takes time resists even being created. We are in the "now generation." We all want stuff yesterday. We want it fast, but we don't understand that some things take time. There is no way around it. Habits that are created in haste and implemented in haste typically do not endure; there is no follow-through and they don't become good, life-affirming habits.

When you are looking to create a new habit, take some time to think it through and plan for it. First, make sure it aligns with what you want to represent your life. Then create some intentional space for the habit in your life. Create time. Create a rhythm. Create the habit in a position of your everyday life that you can repeat. Sometimes it's easy to do things first thing in the morning; sometimes it's the last thing at night, or maybe it's always at lunch, or it's at 9 a.m. that seems to work best for you. It doesn't matter when that time is; what's important is that you can create a consistency around it. Living a habit at a consistent time or a consistent position of the day endows it with the power to survive the challenges that flow into your life every day.

CHAPTER 10:

Internal Conflict Resolution

Happiness will always elude us when our actions are in conflict with our philosophy and principles. This is true both in business and in life in general. Too many times, we engage in activities or with people who clash with our principles; they drain us of our energy to carry out our purpose. We must set these people free and stop engaging in the detrimental behaviors that suck the good out of our lives. Our first step here is to identify those actions and people; then to set an acceptable policy for interacting with them, when necessary; and, finally, to remove from our lives those who do not conform to our rules, written or otherwise.

One of the best examples of someone who lived in perfect alignment AND in complete conflict was Steve Jobs. Dr. Gentempo broke it down best. "A great example would be Steve Job in both positive and negative. Where he was very clear on his value what on his business life with Apple where they basically defined their entire company with one sheet of paper where they defined their values but where he was contradictory and inconsistent with his values was in his personal life and you can see what it cost him there. When applying philosophy in categories of your life it can make amazing things happens and when you're not applying it, it can lead to destruction"

Establishing Rules

For the most part, when you get trampled in life, it's because you did not set up appropriate barriers. When you are offended, it's because you did not make clear the rules of engagement. Setting rules is not about forcing other people to do anything. It's about reinforcing the principles and the values you have set for yourself primarily, and then for others as well. While it's essential to establish rules, this process does not in any way need to include extreme force. Rules can be simple. They can be gentle. They can be expressed through actions as well as words, and they can be implemented in a way that will lead most people to agree with their validity.

How exactly do we do that? You set a rule, first and foremost, by the way in which you act. How you respond to people and situations is one way of setting rules. We create some rules by verbally creating them, by explaining, "This is what I expect." But most rules are established by how we react or what we do in response to some form of stimuli. If somebody insults you and you do nothing, for example, over time that person develops the belief that it's okay to insult you. Conversely, if someone insults you and you correct him or her, politely or not, you are setting a rule. Keep in mind that you do not have to be loud or obnoxious to set a rule. The best rules are set simply and established via consistency.

When setting a rule, you must be consistent or you will simply cause confusion and, perhaps, even become perceived as a hypocrite or insincere. So it's essential to be clear about what your rules really are. I suggest taking some time right now to think about what your rules would be in relation to your values and why they are important. Identifying why they are important will give power to the reason that you are implementing them and consistency with how they are implemented. We'll talk more about setting rules in chapter 15.

Identifying the Offenders

Once your rules are established, you'll undoubtedly find that some violate the rules; we'll call those people "offenders." Typically the most persistent and ardent offender is, actually, ourselves. We set rules around what we would like, but we don't even adhere to them ourselves. Then we respond by beating ourselves up, talking negatively to ourselves, devaluing what we do or what we are. We treat ourselves in ways contrary to how we believe we should be treated. We must focus on understanding that everyone must be accountable—including ourselves.

When identifying outside offenders in our social groups or in our day-to-day lives, it seems almost silly that we should have an entire section dedicated to this subject. At first thought, it seems that we would be able to easily spot the offenders "coming over the wall," as though the offense is so egregious that we cannot help but notice it when it happens.

This could not be farther from the truth. Most encroachments on our rules happen in the form of nudges, in the form of passing comments or actions. We let little things slide because they seem like not that big of a deal. Then we let another breach slide and another and another, and before you know it, we have rules that really mean nothing—rules that have been so bastardized that we do not even know where, when, or how the rule originally was implemented or where we want it to be.

Identifying the offenders happens not in one single large action, but in the repetition of how somebody addresses and treats you. If you start noticing trends, that is when the issue must be addressed. Yes, you might actually need to address that issue within yourself. Give yourself a good sit-down and talking-to!

Addressing the Offenders

Offenses will happen with relative frequency on social media, but that is not the only place these offenders exist. Now that we have identified the offenders, those who are breaking our rules, how exactly do we address them? There are two possibilities: You can either insist that they respect the rules you have set, or you remove them from your life. What is the best way to effectively let people know they are breaking your rules so they can stop the offense? The issue here is one of increasing consequences. Just because somebody steps over a line does not mean we should chop their heads off. That type of overreaction will not build any support for the rule that you are trying to enforce in your life or, for that matter, your company.

The first step always needs to be recognition and acknowledgment of the incident. If somebody calls you a name, for example, if they say you are fat and you take offense, then you must communicate that to them: "Please, do not call me that. I do not appreciate that." In this way, you have communicated the rule, you have communicated the offense, and you have communicated the expectation.

As the second step, you restate the issue, you restate the rule, you restate the comment, and you tell the person you will not allow that to happen again. You have now set a rule of acceptance and non-acceptance. If it happens a third time, you must take more abrupt and aggressive action. Typically, it's a "three strikes and you're out" rule, but that is not hard and fast. The point in addressing the offenders is not for you to make them feel less-than or embarrassed; it is for you to reinforce your rules and stand up for yourself and your rules. If this is the mindset that you take into this scenario, you will not offend anyone that you want to keep in your life. They will respect your standing up for yourself and you will both be better off by communicating with each other.

In the next section, I'll talk about a real-world example of how I addressed this in my world of social networking.

Are You a Healthy Social "Feeder"?

We all know the saying "Garbage in, garbage out," right? We understand that we are what we eat as well, right? With those two rules in mind, let's take a look at the way in which we consume information from social media. I know we're all guilty of it, looking at a post from a friend or associate and scoffing because of a drama that existed within the post. We wonder to ourselves why on earth they post such stuff and why people read it, but then when the next installation to the story is posted, we click again.

What does that do to our internal mental health? Are we supporting a healthy lifestyle by reading that stuff, or are we consuming the junk food of social media? I think we can all agree that reading that and getting involved, however distant, does not advance our personal goals and dreams. There are a great number of psychosocial reasons that we allow ourselves to get drawn to that junk, but I am not here for analysis. I am here to help!

So here is what I did when this issue erupted in my own life. Feel free to adopt any variation of my response that fits for you.

Set criteria.

For me it is the rule of two. If I am reading or even see a post from someone that is laden with drama, I will actually give them a pass. We all have bad days, so sometimes we need to vent, though we can probably agree social media is not the best place for that. If they post a second one in a time frame that I can remember, I simply unfollow. No drama or snotty shot across their bow just choose not to follow.

Invest in positive and rewarding messages.

As fast as I unfollow, I click to follow those who share really good tips, information, and, most important, positive perspectives. This does not mean that I read every one of their posts, but it does mean that if I see one from them, I expect it to fall into one of those categories.

Enjoy and share.

Now when you open your app or site, the Twitter, Facebook, Snapchat, or other feed that hits you square between the eyes, what you see and read empowers you. If you do it right, you should be able to open your feed at any moment for a motivational fix and then jump back to what you were doing with a little more pep! Now that you have received the good news and information, share it! This is the stuff we want to see go viral and let those around you follow the same stuff. Just think, everyone around you reading positive news instead of the negative trash that is out there.

Keep your house clean.

Finally, and most important, you must be vigilant about keeping your feeds clean from those who wish to spew garbage. Do not worry that you made a mistake by following someone who ended up being negative or cruel. Simply click "unfollow" and do this on a regular basis to avoid needing to "clean house" by starting all over.

I love my social media feeds because they empower, challenge, and encourage me. I am so glad I recognized the need to keep my own feeds positive and uplifting, because I have been so much happier and positive myself since making this little change.

Potential Areas of Conflict Ahead

As you begin to state your rules and, even more important, strongly stand up for them, you will actually create more conflict. Remember, friction exists because two opposing forces rub against each other. That can mean that one of those opposing forces is standing firm and the other is moving in the opposite direction. When you stand firm, there will be people who resist, causing friction. That is okay as long as you once again strongly communicate your rules and expectations. Do not see this conflict as a negative, but rather as an opportunity to express your personal beliefs and live your personal values. As you define your conflicts, you will also begin to better define those who support you and those who are there to help. When you take a stand this way a leader, you not only define the expectations for those who work with you; you also inspire them by your example and help them to create healthy boundaries that enrich their own lives.

Part 3: Peace Surrounds You

CHAPTER 11:

Define and Appreciate Your Support Network

We will go through tough times, times we where do not even believe in ourselves. Those are dangerous times—especially for someone tasked with leading others—and it is at these times that our support network is so important. Most likely, this support has helped us get through the tough times we have already experienced. In this chapter, we will take the time to reflect and recognize who our supporters have been and then consider ways that we can thank them and truly appreciate them going forward.

Reflect on the Challenges Already Conquered

When we are considering how to conquer a challenge before us, the most effective way is to consider the challenges we have already conquered in the past. These successes prove that we are strong and capable, perhaps more so than we realize at the moment. So, we must look at our past and appreciate our achievements, because it is through recognizing these successes that we are able to develop a game plan to address whatever might lie ahead.

Reflection is an important part of developing a strategy. So many of us approach challenges reactively and begin to strategize without laying down the essential groundwork that comes with reflection. Such reflection allows us to absorb not just the information in front of us, but the information within us. That helps us understand that we may already have the strength we need, strength we did not even realize was there. When developing a response to a situation or preparing to part with an employee, for example, reflection is paramount to success, and it must not be overlooked.

Recognize Who Was There

When we reflect on challenges that we have overcome, it's helpful to broaden our scope and consider more than just ourselves in that situation. By doing so we will recognize people who have supported us, people who have encouraged us, those who challenged us, and those who have just been there for us in any number of ways. It is those individuals to whom we must appreciate and recognize. When we create a team, we want team members who will go to battle with us, who will be there during the tough times, who will say in the face of challenge, "I got this" or "I have your back." The best way to assess who will be there in the future is to consider the people who have done this for us in the past. Past actions give credibility to their words.

There are different levels of "being there," and the need that you have for each person may be different. Sometimes what you need is simply a passive supportive person; at other times, you need somebody to actively step up. Recognize who they've been and what they've done; then seek them out—these are the team members you need. Instead of feeling burdened, they may feel flattered, even honored, at your request for their help. The ability to show true vulnerability and acknowledge that you need others is critical to your own development, as well as theirs and that of your organization.

Small Gestures, Huge Impact

When we recognize the people who have been there for us during our challenges, one of the first things we think of is to say "thank you." Yet often we are so caught up in the situation, we forget to do even that, or we just don't make time to say that simple phrase. Then later we think about it and we can't decide what is a big enough deed to truly convey our gratitude. What we miss is that most people would prefer smaller gestures with higher repetition and consistency than large gestures with sparse frequency.

The human psyche needs to be constantly reminded of what it's doing and why. When we receive constant support—in the form of little thank-you's, small gifts, simple acknowledgments of our efforts—it has a huge impact on the effort we put forward in the future. This also affects both personal and organizational relationships. Buy-in is much easier when people know they will be recognized, even if it is on a small scale. This does not mean you should not ever show your appreciation in a grand way, but do not miss all the opportunities to show your gratitude in smaller, everyday gestures.

Make the Time to Show Appreciation

As we just discussed, we often fail to find the time to even tell people "thank you." Now, I am suggesting that you take accountability and create the intention to make the time to show your appreciation; don't just expect the opportunity to show up. Time is the most valuable resource in any relationship and in any organization. It is one that cannot be manipulated; it cannot be collected; and it cannot be saved. If you do not use the opportunity when it is there, it passes, never to be seen again.

Making time requires action; if you do not make the time or take the time, then you will not be able to simply find the time. This is similar to the way in which we say we do not have time to work out or to donate to recreational activities. (I think we all struggle with this.) For those who cannot find time and organize their priorities and create these intentions, this will be a lifelong battle. Developing the habit of making time to do the little things will benefit you in numerous ways. When you have the technique and skills to create time and use time effectively, then when the important stuff—really big stuff—happens, you will be able to attend to it appropriately because you will know how to manage your time.

As Dale Brown, legendary head basketball coach for Louisiana State University (LSU) says: "The most important thing about leadership is that the people do not care what you know until they know you care. As was stated in Booker T Washington's book on leadership he said the job of a leader is to get the people to think more of the leader but the purpose of a great leader is to get the people to think more of themselves"

So where to start? Try this: Take a piece of paper and write down five names of people you need to thank for helping you through a tough spot. Then go to your calendar (on your computer, phone, or planner—they all work) and pick a time *every* day of the work week that you can consistently mark off for this important action. (For example, first thing in the morning at home, right after lunch, just before lunch, mid-afternoon.) Write "Thank someone" on that spot on your calendar. Then look at that list and text, call, send an email, write a letter, send a smoke signal if necessary—just do it. *Every* day! Little habits, huge results. This is how it is done. Next, imagine how this same process can help you with other things you "need to be better at." No magic, no easy answer.

CHAPTER 12:

Share Your Vision

Sometimes it is scary, but we must be fearless and shout our vision to the world. By sharing our vision, we attract those who want to support us and our ideas. Proclaiming and clarifying your vision is also a way to guide the people you lead even when you are not in front of them. This chapter will describe, first, how to create your personal vision and then how to share it with your team and others.

Creating Your Vision

This is a watershed moment for any leader. As we touched on in chapter 7, creating your vision and writing it down takes all the dreams you have had and begins to give them form. Please do not underestimate the power of these acts. We all have dreams and hopes and wishes, but to have a vision is something much different.

How does a vision differ from a dream? A vision is structured—it includes a distinct destination and outlines a path. We may not know the specifics of that path at first, but we have "awoken" to the realization that certain things need to happen and a series of events need to occur for our dream to become a reality. This realization typically becomes a moment of clarity, empowerment, and, let's face it, sheer terror! It is the difference between dreaming that someday you would like to climb

Mount Kilimanjaro and standing at the base of the mountain gazing up at the peak.

Here's a short exercise to help you with this process. First, take each of your values and write down what it would look like if you truly lived that value for the rest of your life or career. If you already have a vision, match it up with what comes out of this process—it should look pretty close. Then take what you have come up with as far as results and just start brainstorming things that would need to happen for your dream to become a reality; whose help you will need to engage, and what challenges you might have to overcome.

This process will move you closer to defining your vision. Your vision should be a culmination of you living your values, principles, and philosophy. When it is created in this first stage, it is a beautiful thing. Know that the more integrity, vulnerability, and authenticity you put into it, the better your vision will stand the test of time and allow for growth. Once you have a working model, it is time to give it the truest power. Share it!

What Should I Share?

What to share is always a difficult question. We want to show people the positives, but often are reluctant to reveal the valleys that we know will happen on the path to our vision. In this area, tough as it may be, I suggest transparency and authenticity. Everybody knows there will be valleys and everybody knows there will be peaks. What people fear the most is what they don't know. People generally are resilient and can find ways to get through many different obstacles, but the toughest obstacle to overcome is uncertainty—not knowing what is around the next bend. Plus, others will more than likely smell when you are not telling the whole truth.

When sharing your vision with the people you lead, the most important thing to share is your ultimate goal and their role in it, so they can always keep their eye on the prize while understanding their value in the process. By sharing this, as well as your concerns, you are allowing your team members to feel part of the process, and that is true power. When you take the time to explain the process you are going through, as well as your concerns or doubts, they understand that their efforts and their thoughts are valuable and desired. They recognize that they can be an important part of this vision. A perfect vision with no valleys—no obstacles to climb over—is just a rule to follow, not a cause to be a part of.

Now let me pose a caveat: As a leader, you have your own internal roller coaster. Sometimes you have irrational fears or overexcited possibilities. Make sure you have run your vision through the "process" several times before sharing and then start with your closest advisers and LISTEN to their thoughts and concerns while keeping the faith in your possibilities.

How to Share

Sometimes it is tough to know how to share your vision: Is it a big speech? Is it a company mission? Is it a slogan? Here's the truth: The best way to share is straight from the heart. Being honest and authentic and vulnerable, as we talked about in our discussion of what to share, the how-to-share follows in much the same way. In sharing your vision, by not creating an image of invincibility, you recognize the humanity of people and welcome them as participants in realizing your vision. Also, the act of sharing the amazing possibilities allows them to dream alongside you. That is of great value. Sharing your vision often and consistently is also extremely important, but the only way to do that is to truly know your vision for yourself. Before you share, make sure you are confident in what you feel—not necessarily in the exact process of how you will reach your vision, but in how you see the process from where you currently stand.

So now that I have explained the basics on how to share, what is the best tool or medium to share this vision? That's easy . . . values!

CHAPTER 13:

Managing Up—Values as a Communications Tool

Perhaps more than anything else, our values constitute the heart of most of our communications. Through understanding and honoring our own values, we define how we can communicate in a professional and honest way as we confront exciting, challenging, and even difficult situations. Building on that, by understanding our team values, we can communicate to our team what is our most important objective and how we want to work toward accomplishing that goal. It is when we consistently communicate through our values that we create a common platform of information and understanding—a platform that ultimately increases our effectiveness while staying true to who we are and how we want to lead.

How to Use Our Values

Once we have established our most important values, we can convey them consistently and effectively through our various forms of communication. We communicate in accordance with those values. This includes making an effort to truly understand what others are communicating to us and what values are important to them. This is all part of how we establish a level of respect in our relationships. If you respect others' values and understand what is important to them, it is much easier to communicate what you want by relating your objective to their values. For example, if family is important to some of your team members and one of your values is productivity, you could communicate to them that you want them to improve their productivity so they can spend more time with their families. This is just an example, but you can see how understanding their values first can avoid a very painful situation and result in positive, rather than negative action.

A really cool thing happens once we finally define our values and commit ourselves to living by them. Our communication is elevated to a level of respect. No longer do we see value in degrading others. No longer do we take a negative approach with our communications. We communicate on a level that seeks to enhance, to enrich the values that others live by, and we use the next task as an opportunity to make that values based life better. By understanding your values and their values, you can also anticipate areas of potential conflict. You can foresee an issue that may arise based on values and prepare to deal with it before you ever need to have the actual conversation. If you address such issues proactively, the recipient feels heard and the chances of a positive response increases substantially. This does not mean that we do not ever make mistakes or act out of disrespect. But when that happens, we do recognize the incongruence much faster and have the humbleness to ask for forgiveness and learn from our mistakes.

Team/Organization Values

While acting in accordance with our individual values is essential for communicating based on a level of respect, keeping our team or shared values at the forefront takes it all to a much greater level. When we communicate based on values that have been already established as being shared, we can move toward implementing those values throughout our organization. The power that exists here comes from shared responsibility and strength. In the previous chapters, we identified the importance of individual values and ways to go about identifying them. But how do we define team values? These can be established in a couple different ways. If the team is new to the idea of deliberating on values, you may want to take action, as the leader, and establish which values are the most important for the team and then work toward creating understanding about this objective.

Once team members understand that the team values are a shared collection of all participants' values, buy-in will result. Team members have a cohesive bond when they recognize that we are all accountable for living toward those values. When this happens, a level of support is created that allows the team to overcome difficult situations and see possibilities beyond what would exist with only individual actions.

Managing Up

One of the most important concepts in this entire book is what I call "managing up." This refers to our overall goal for the people we lead: to achieve greatness, not avoid mistakes. Mistakes will happen, but we want our team members to focus on being great. When someone makes a mistake, how we respond is critical. Certainly, the individual must understand what the mistake was, but our reaction needs to be forward-looking and positive, because to rehash the mistake offers no productive value for the future. Let's examine a common mistake that could happen in virtually any setting: Somebody knocks a glass off the counter and it shatters. If the mistake resulted from a lack of attention to detail, then we should let the person know that they need to pay more attention and ask them to commit to that. If we respond by saying, "Why did you do that? What were you thinking? Where were you at?" that doesn't help the person to not break the glass. It doesn't put the glass back together. If our response takes an analytical stance, where the individual is brought to understand the cause of the mistake, that can have some value—but it must be done with an eye toward deciding what you will do with that information. (What did you learn from that experience to help you have a better outcome in the future?) Helping people focus on what they need to do next—not what they didn't do earlier—helps them move forward positively and understand that what's important is to improve and get better; again, it's not about avoiding mistakes. If we stay stuck in the realm of avoiding mistakes, we become shell-shocked and we don't make any decisions. We definitely do not benefit from that.

In this area, here is one way you can lead by example as I discussed in my blog.

Be a Fire Not a Flashlight

Quote of the Week: "Be the Light"

Have you ever seen one of those reality competition shows where someone comes in and tells the contestant everything they did wrong with their project? (Structure, tattoo, food, etc.) Do you ever wonder if there was another approach that would be better?

I was listening to someone talk about all the darkness and evil in the world and shining a flashlight on how people need to address the darkness in their lives. It got me to thinking about how we tend to look at our problems, challenges, and sins. We tend to approach them like an out-of-body mechanic repairing our wrongs or perceived defects.

I also noticed we sometimes go through life like that, pointing the flashlight of enlightenment on what we see as wrong in the world. It did not sit well with me and I asked, "How do I help people see that there is another way?" In my Expecting Greatness program, one of the first things I teach is that for the program to work in your life, you have to be committed to being the example. In reflecting on that, the solution became clear.

Be a Fire, not a Flashlight.

A flashlight, while effective, only points out things surrounded by darkness. A fire, on the other hand, can be added to a torch or lighthouse, and it attracts and guides people and fills the world with light in all directions. Taking away all the symbolism, you can see that by living your life in a good way and treating others in a good way, you allow them to watch and then make their own improvements because they like what they see. When they own the change, it becomes much more permanent and powerful in their lives.

Remember the last time you watched a video or someone in person do something you admired and maybe even brought you to tears? How did it make you feel? What did it make you want to do? Now it may not have been enough to push you into action (baby steps!) but if you were surrounded by that, how might you act differently?

Be that example, that light. Be that fire.

Never Fear Failure

"Failing forward" is a concept and phrase that had been around for a while. Thomas J Watson, former CEO of IBM, said, "If you want to increase your success rate, double your rate of failure." Everyone from John Wooden to Jack Canfield to Ellen DeGeneres have quotes about putting failure into perspective, yet most of us fear the word like the plague. Why?

From what I have deduced, it comes down to our upbringing and, more specifically, events and how we reacted to them when we were young. If you think back to when you were young, what type of events were the words "fail" or "failure" tied to? They were typically used in some catastrophic yet relative way. Look at grading in school, for example. You may fail to get an A or 100 percent, but we do not use that word until we hit the bottom of the barrel—when we get a big fat F. Even when we are motivated, we are urged to do something so we do not become a failure, which is referred to as being at the bottom of the barrel, down and out.

Had we seen smaller mistakes as fails and treated them as learning opportunities—where we are safe to reassess our approach and learn what we missed or mistook—there would be a vastly different approach to this concept. And, I would venture to say that we would ultimately advance to our goal much faster and efficiently.

Being at Peace with Decisions

When we make a decision, we must make the best decision we can based on the information at hand. A good decision is good when it is based on the information available, not based on the results. We all make mistakes and we all have times when certain issues later come up that had not been previously known or seen, but that would have affected our decision. For example, say you decide to support a certain cause or charity, and then discover that the organization manipulated, mishandled or misused the money it in some way. It's not that you have made an erroneous decision. The decision to support that group was not wrong, because you did not have advanced information that this would happen. There might be regret for what the group did with the money, but that had nothing to do with your decision to support the charity. In the same way, we cannot say the decision was a good one just because the outcome ended up being positive, if that was indeed the case.

This does not mean we do not take risks. It means that the decision must be separated from the result. Once we understand this separation, then we can understand that all decisions must be made in accordance with our values. The values must be the filter through which we evaluate our options. They are how we reached a decision, not the results that may have materialized. Acting and making decisions based on our values will give us a much longer-run vision and allow us to be strategic about our future and our long-term success.

Having peace with our decisions is a key sign that we are leading from a place of peace. As you can see, your decisions are a result of your values, not the beginning of them. If we can confidentially trace our decision back to our most important values and the decision aligns with those values, it is tough not to have peace with the decision.

CHAPTER 14:

The WIIFM Principle

There used to be a time when people did a job just because it was the job, and honor existed in the performance. It did not matter if you were a CEO or the garbage collector. Those days are gone. This does not mean people do not take pride in their work anymore. It means that instead of doing the job well and then expecting reward, people want to know more of the endgame up front. They want to know: What's in it for me? or WIIFM? This concept can drive supervisors and leaders mad with anger. "How dare you ask me when a raise is coming before day 1?" We have all had those thoughts, but today's followers want that path defined for them. You can either react with anger and keep losing employees, or you can answer their questions and make them part of the process in deciding if this job will work for them. This does not mean that you will have to change the core values or key elements of the position; it means you must communicate your vision for the position, explaining the opportunities available—and that ain't all bad!

The Way It Was and the Way It Is

When we start to talk about our parents and grandparents, and the way in which they worked and the philosophies by which they worked, we quickly realize how different those generations were from what we see in people today. We also must appreciate that we are different from our parents or grandparents, but yet not see ourselves as a lazy, entitled generation. It always seems to be the next generation that is deserving of such criticisms. Perspective is an important thing to keep in mind when discussing the situation. Change is constant and will always be constant. Disagreement regarding the best way to implement a process will always happen. We all remember the past in slightly different ways, but I remind people that our memories will always be much fonder than reality.

When we look at the past, it's important to respect the way it was, but it's also important to recognize that that is the end of it. That is the way it *was*. What is important now is dealing with the way it *is*. There might be things we do not like. There might be prractices and beliefs of today's generation with which we struggle, but that is the way it is and it is the environment in which we must work. If we do not adapt with the youth of today and, more important, with the youth of tomorrow, we will not be effective leaders. Effective leaders need not be trendy, but they must be current, and they do have to be able to relate to those whom they must lead. It is and can be a difficult challenge for many.

The WIIFM Perspective

People with the WIIFM perspective do not believe that what they are asking for is outlandish or unrealistic. They believe, much as they have been taught, that you only get what you ask for. The fact that they decide to ask early seems really inconsequential to them. The fact that they want the pat on the back, even the payoff, almost instantaneously—or before they have done any work—might be frustrating for those of us who are leaders, but it is the way many act or respond to challenge and opportunity today. According to the WIIFM perspective, it is not disrespect they intend to convey upon the task, person, or the company; they simply have a desire to understand what the road map looks like further ahead.

Part of the challenge is that many companies have degraded their own level of honor and thus the faith that employees have in them. Now is the day of asking for money up front to guarantee that the employee won't be eventually screwed over. The WIIFM perspective is part protectionist and part visionary. In fact, those with this perspective simply want to know where they are going and they want some form of commitment from us before they start down the path of their new job. To a degree, this perspective and approach is very insightful and open-eyed, but it also flies in the face of what we historically considered appropriate.

Why Do We Have to Flex with Them?

When we think about the way things were, the way things are, and the way things may be, sometimes we ask ourselves, "Why do we have to change? Why can't we hold on to our old ways?" Those are very good and challenging questions. In certain areas, we must make very intentional decisions regarding which side of the conversation we are working. I like to use the quote from Thomas Jefferson when trying to gauge myself here. He said, "In matters of conscience, stand like a rock. In matters of fashion, go with the flow." When it comes to how we will manage our team, we must understand what has to be done, as it aligns with the vision of the company. This cannot be adjusted impulsively or on a daily basis. However, the way in which we get it done can be more flexible. The fact that somebody is asking us or challenging us to look at our operations in a different way is not always a negative.

If we approach these opportunities with respect, we may find some true gems. Let me explain. When employees challenge us about how to do something or when they will get paid, we must respect them and recognize that they are trying to do the same thing we are: to make the best world they can for themselves and their families; in fact for everybody with whom they come into contact. If we respect that as an initial premise, then we can look at their question from a different perspective and give it greater credibility. Just because they want to help people in a different way does not mean that they don't want to help people. If we respect that, then we can come to a position of understanding. Now, at the end we may still disagree, but we will find a new level of respect.

A Future Look at Successfully Working with WIIFM

As we look forward and try to navigate the new management style while understanding this perspective, we need to ask several questions: What does it look like? How does it influence the way we do business? One big advantage to working with the WIIFM principle comes when we understand that if someone comes to us with a question; it is respectful and appropriate for us to respond with our own question as well. For example, if an employee asks, "How will I get paid?" there is nothing wrong with responding with the question, "How will you earn it?" If they want a road map of compensation or promotion, then they should provide a road map of accomplishments. If this back-and-forth is used as a powerful, uplifting conversation, it is extremely beneficial. If it is used as a condescending justification, or as a way of putting someone else in their place, then it will have a negative outcome.

If we look at WIIFM as merely giving everyone five-year road maps, then we are all better prepared for the challenges and opportunities the future may bring. When, as an employer, I first encountered the WIIFM principle, I was very frustrated. But as I learned to understand where it came from and appreciated it, I was able to provide my employees with a more detailed perspective on their future while they gave me a more detailed estimation on how they would accomplish that future. From something that started out as a very negative concept, we have developed something very powerful and forward-thinking.

CHAPTER 15:

Creating a Peaceful Environment

Peaceful leadership flourishes in the right environment, but that environment does not just magically appear. You must create it. Living from your values helps create the environment necessary for effective, honest communication. Managing the landscape of people, energy, rules, and respect will all help generate the ideal work environment. This chapter sets the groundwork for recruiting and developing employees who will help you achieve your vision of a successful environment.

Your Vision of the Environment

Your vision of the ideal work environment is ultimately important because it makes the entire buy-in process possible. When creating your vision for this environment, it must be based on your values and principles that can be supported by others to make the vision a reality. What I'm talking about here is the fact that sometimes we have a vision, but we do not carry out the actions needed to support that vision or make it become a reality.

This is not uncommon, and it happens when we create visions out of arbitrary or ungrounded situations. If we dream without having a logical strategy for how we will execute the plan, then our dreams can look like anything, but they will not come to fruition unless we have a detailed vision of our goals.

When creating your vision, look back at your values; look back at your habits; and look at how you can create an environment rooted in what your actions already are. The people you surround yourself with to help you bring your vision to life should really just be an enhancement, completion, or complement to your existing vision. A vision should represent you, and you should represent your vision.

More Rule Setting

Part of creating an environment or culture where you can lead from a place of peace involves establishing some "rules," or guidelines for your interactions. We talked about this in chapter 10, but now we're going to focus on how rules contribute to the environment you are trying to create. The first rule that must be set in this regard is "respect." Of all the rules that you decide to create to help establish structure and organization, respect is the one that is the most foundational, and really is the key. Without respect, you will not have a peaceful environment, nor will you have quality conversation, communication, direction, or debate. These are the things that you must have to create greatness. Without respect, you will accomplish nothing of substance that will last, or truly change the world for good. Respect is pivotal. When respect is a foundation of yourself, your company or organization, and others in your world, then you can accomplish amazing things.

If you enter into a conversation and realize that the other party also wants to do good, and make the world a better place through their vision of what the world looks like, amazingly powerful discussions will occur.

Our challenge is that we tend to disrespect the other person's vision if it looks different from our own. We treat it as if it were wrong. But it's not wrong; it's just different. Yes, there are times when we must stand our ground and say that something is wrong for us and contrary to our beliefs. That is completely okay and would make Thomas Jefferson proud. His statement on when we must stand firm and when we should compromise guides our actions. Be respectful, especially to your own principles.

From the foundation of respect, you move on to establish rules on acceptance. This means that you are the gatekeeper of the actions that will be allowed. The rules you create are not intended to control but empower. By setting rules that align with your and your organization's values, you are providing guidance for all to follow, and creating an environment that supports and fosters a culture that can buy into something greater than any one individual.

When looking to reward employees, we want to identify greatness in their actions, not just in their results. When we judge by results only, we fail to recognize the numerous external factors that must come together for the desired result to happen, including successful and positive actions. The integrity and the intention of the employee is in itself worthy of recognition. As leaders, we must hunt for these values within our organization, as they are the most important component of the entire company.

When we celebrate that our values that are being lived by our people within the company, it demonstrates that this is a good deed and is what it takes to be recognized within the company. Whatever you recognize is what gets supported. That is true from a positive standpoint *and* a negative standpoint. If people watch others cheating, stealing, being dishonest, and getting ahead because of it, then they are more likely to conclude that that is the only way to get ahead, and they will either join in or, if their values conflict with this and those values are vitally important to them, they will leave. If we focus our light on positive actions and do not only reward the results, we increase the chance of achieving success in a healthy manner.

Obviously, every company has good and bad elements, as does every person. We must remember that our company is much like the Cherokee Indian tale of two wolves. It goes like this:

One evening, an elderly Cherokee brave told his grandson about a battle that goes on inside people. He said, "My son, the battle is between two wolves inside all of us. One is evil. It is anger, envy, jealousy, sorrow, regret, greed, arrogance, self-pity, guilt, resentment, inferiority, lies, false pride, superiority, and ego. The other is good. It is joy, peace, love, hope, serenity, humility, kindness, benevolence, empathy, generosity, truth, compassion and faith."

The grandson thought about it for a minute and then asked his grandfather, "Which wolf wins?" The old Cherokee simply replied, "The one that you feed."

In the same way that we feed the good or the bad wolf inside us, we feed the good or the bad wolf within our organization. The effects of the bad wolf or the bad elements succeeding in our company cause poor employee morale, disengagement, frustration, anger, stealing, cheating, and lying while the good elements create an amazing future for all of us.

The good elements create unity, sharing, and success of the truest nature. The "wolf" that will win is the one that we support as leaders. If we see bad elements, we can't just let them grow. We must address them. If we see good elements growing, we must recognize them and nurture them so they will grow even more. It is our responsibility as leaders to help the greatness grow.

Create It from the Ground Level in the Weeds

The culture that we all want to create does not come into being by us, in one booming voice, declaring the new world order. Rather, it happens when we instill at the ground level the little things that need to be done—like living by example and supporting and rewarding the actions that need to be accomplished. If our team sees us do these things day after day after day, they will begin to assimilate the same expectations into their own lives, into their ground-level actions.

Too often, we put out declarations or create posters that relay a Utopian perspective of how the world should work without full consideration of how we are supposed to live. Values, ideas, and concepts mean nothing if we can't live them. Where we live them is at the ground level and in the weeds. It's between the meetings that life really exists. It's between the motivational speakers that we grow our company. It's between the retreats that we really bond.

Establishing a Leaders Council

The establishment of a leaders council is an important step in creating a healthy and peaceful work environment, because it allows your message and values to be disseminated from not just one person but from many. If your organization becomes optimized, the message travels from the bottom up, from side to side, and from the top down.

The consistency of the message will be evident when you see everyone working together toward the same goal. It is sometimes difficult to understand exactly how this synergy works, and for each organization, it will be a little different, but you will know it when you see it. The leaders council will help you bring together a core of thinkers who understand the vision and the values, and then are able to disseminate them to their respective departments. Note that this is not the management team, but a selection of personnel from across the organization. It may or may not contain the entire management team.

CHAPTER 16:

Effective versus Efficient

As technology advances, the struggle between effectiveness and efficiency looms larger and becomes ever more prevalent. Think about your smartphone. This nifty tool offers a plethora of examples where we must ride the fine line between effectiveness and efficiency. The phone's capabilities are very efficient; that would be tough to deny. The ability to transmit our voices digitally through the air to almost anywhere in the world, to be able to do business while waiting for a latte, to be able to ask Google any obscure questions and receive a response within milliseconds, to be able to connect in so many ways that we haven't even imagined—all of these capabilities demonstrate the phone's efficiency. But, is it effective? That depends on the user.

There is a great saying that says "sometimes we are so busy *doing* that we forget to stop and ask if we *should*." When we load up our smartphone with apps, tools, and contacts, we do it because we can, and the phone can efficiently handle it. But does this result in us being more effective in our lives? I think we can all see times where we fell into the rabbit hole and then stopped to ask, "What the heck am I doing? This is a waste of time!" It typically begins innocently enough; it was a simple and efficient action or development, but in the end it was not an effective use of your time and, as a result, became a negative influence.

The primary issue here is the desire for short-term returns without proper respect for long-term vision. That does not mean you should never have fun or partake in less-than-serious activities and appear frivolous. Your mind and body need that break from the relentless pursuit of efficiency and effectiveness. It is the extremes that become dangerous and interfere with the realization of your long-term vision. Short-term payoff does not appreciate the sacrifice required or the immensity and longevity of the challenge.

When I was training for my climb of Mount Kilimanjaro, I noticed in the brochure a caution that on some of the days it would take five hours to go three miles. I thought, "Heck, I hike three and a half miles in a single hour on the treadmill at 12 percent grade. Why so slow?" Then as I thought about it, I realized the intensity and scale of my trek. I gained instant respect for the challenge that I was about to undertake.

We must be cautious to avoid getting caught up in the zeitgeist of "faster is better." We are continuously making concessions of quality for the illusion of speed and efficiency. When striving to make yourself or your organization more efficient, know that if you sacrifice quality, you will find yourself efficiently out of a job or business. It does not occur like a sonic boom but in the culmination of all the small decisions made many times a day. That is why it is so important to know the difference between being efficient and effective. Peace can only come with effectiveness.

Defining the Difference

Words carry extreme power and sometimes have multiple interpretations. "Efficient" is one such term. Dictionary.com defines it as "performing or functioning in the best possible manner with the least waste of time and effort; having and using requisite knowledge, skill, and industry" and "utilizing a particular commodity or product with the least waste of resources or effort."

Even in this definition there is confusion. The first iteration includes the phrase "best possible manner," which goes beyond the "least waste" and begins to imply accurate direction and results. Ambiguous and relative terms like "best" tend to have that effect. When it comes to efficient, the purest definition refers to the lack of waste and the height of expediency, and it is in that where efficient and effective differ so fundamentally.

The *Hindenburg* burned with extreme efficiency; that is something nobody can deny. And if death and destruction were the desired end result, then it would have been effective as well. But just because something happens with efficiency does not make it effective, and just because it is effective does not make it good. Without intentional action, meaningful strides toward the desired goal are not possible and we end up efficiently wasting resources.

As I lay out the treacherous nature of implementing efficiency, I do not mean to say that it is inherently bad. An effective model without the proper degree of efficiency is just an idea, and I do not know anyone who changed the world with an unimplemented idea. Efficiently moving toward a direction or goal is what creates true value for everyone.

Recognizing and Resisting the "Efficient Pull"

It is easy, it is the path well-traveled, the allure of short-term gain, and it seems to make sense. The pull of efficiency is strengthened by all these characteristics, and if we observe someone else taking the efficient path and experiencing good short-term results, it becomes even tougher to stay on the path and pace we know is going to be effective over the long term. The classic tale of the tortoise and the hare is applicable here, and I want to illuminate some attributes and qualities for which the tortoise deserves credit.

First, know thyself! What a great example! The tortoise realizes that he is not a hare and that if he attempts to push himself at breakneck speed, not only will he fail to keep up with the hare, but he will utterly exhaust his energy reserves—and that will prevent him from carrying on at his predetermined optimal speed.

Second, let the Jones be the Jones. When the hare took off, it appeared as though the tortoise did not even recognize or care about the blistering pace at which the hare accelerated. He stayed focused on his task and his pace. Finally, he did not incite the hare when he passed him by. He did not allow his anger and adrenaline to provoke the hare into rejoining the race at an ultra-committed level determined to show up the trash-talking tortoise. No, the tortoise just stayed focused on his task and his pace.

As a leader, you will have many people, demands, and opportunities attempting to distract you from your committed course, wanting to pull you to a path of ease but not righteousness. It is this pull you must resist; stay the course and ensure that your actions are founded on values, principles, and habits that align. Know who you and your organization is, and supports that identity. Do not waste energy and resources chasing others or trends that do not correspond with your values.

As you strive to continue on this path, make use of the most powerful tool you have: your vision of what is possible. That also is what will attract and give those whom you lead a reason to hope. It is powerful, indeed.

CHAPTER 17

Hire Slow, Fire Fast

In this chapter, we'll discuss the importance of establishing a thorough hiring process to assure that potential employees' values align with your own, and therefore will contribute to the positive culture and team you are creating. If a current employee is not supporting or aligning with your values, then that person needs to go. First though, you must appreciate the work they have done and understand the void that will create when they leave. We will also examine the negative effect that drama and rumors can have on an otherwise positive work environment. When employees are creating issues, often it is because of their own unhappiness in the position, and we need to liberate them from their own hell for the good of the entire enterprise.

Find and Fire Based on Values

Who are these Negative Neds and Nancies that we need to eradicate from our business? How do we find them? Do they stand up and say, "Here I am"? No, we know that's not the case. The way to find them is to look for team members who do not adhere to, or continually buck the company's values. Generally, they do this because they disagree with or are not in support of those values, and because they just cannot relate to that value system. These people are unhappy because they are required to do something instead of getting to do what they prefer; they vehemently resist the value that they are required to embrace or the rule that they are required to follow.

These employees will stick out in your organization. When you ask other employees to list someone who does not follow the company's values, you'll find the same names keep coming up. This is not about taking someone to the woodshed. Rather, this is about releasing them from the pain that they experience from trying to force themselves into a structure that is foreign and distressing to them. Too many times, people stay in positions that make them very uncomfortable and unhappy simply because they fear the unknown.

This fact helps explain why we have such a low engagement factor in so many of our businesses. By identifying these employees and acknowledging on both sides that they are not in congruence with the organization's values, they will see the wisdom of moving on. In the end, they will likely be relieved that you are releasing them and giving them the way out that they could not muster the courage to take on their own.

Estimate the Impact

It is important to think carefully before pulling any triggers in business or in life, before taking actions that are irrevocable. This occasion is no different. When we are looking at letting an employee go, we must first review what tasks the person does and assess the impact of having that employee's tasks heaped upon another employee for a certain amount of time. If we don't understand the impact up front, then firing someone may actually cause more headaches for ourselves than we ever thought possible.

By truly understanding and appreciating what work this person did, we can acknowledge those who will have to pick up the slack. If you give people a heads-up, they are often much more willing to step up and take on the added responsibility for the needed period of time.

Assess and Repair the Damage

One of the things that is difficult to comprehend is just how much damage a negative person can create in an organization. Drama is a noisy magnet, and it will bring out all of the noisiness that exists within other people as well. When this person—this tornado—comes through our offices, they often do not leave quietly, and they may even leave a path of destruction. It's important to assess the level of damage done by this negativity and then to proactively take steps to repair that damage.

In chapter 14, we talked about the WIIFM? (What's in It for Me?) principle. According to this principle, people are driven to ask that self-focused question, "Why am I here—what is my purpose in doing this?" While leaders may initially feel quite frustrated that their team members are asking this question, it is actually a very powerful and reassuring question because it indicates that the person cares about the big picture of the company. They want to use their energies in a way that aligns with their values, and they want to ensure that they are indeed a good fit with your organization. Related to this is the way that you can begin repairing the damage done by a negative employee. This happens indirectly when you ensure that the expectations you hold, and those of your team, align with the company values, as well as the employees' personal values. This harmony will enhance employee buy-in and go far in contributing to your organization's eventual success.

Set Expectations on Actions and Expect Excellence

When we are setting our expectations, we should set them based on what can be controlled. To not do this creates an external locus of control that becomes frustrating for all involved. For example, if I were to tell you that I expect you to not have it rain today, you would feel hopeless because you obviously can't control the weather. On the other hand, if my expectation was that you bring an umbrella, then that is something you can do.

By putting the expectations on the actions that can be controlled, I've empowered you and have enabled you to be successful in your endeavors. When we expect excellence on actions, this means that we do not accept second-rate performance. If we ask people to treat others with respect, we must draw a firm line, because this expectation is based on their actions. If they are disrespectful to others, we cannot let it slide because they can control that action. When we tell someone that they need to be on time every time, they know that actions like planning ahead will be required to prepare for unexpected obstacles and delays. As long as they do this—as long as they have carried out every logical action to prepare—we can work with any result that is truly out of their control. The expectation is about their actions.

We all know there will be some exceptions to the rule, but they must be very rare. The more you believe in and communicate these values, the less often you will have to ever deal with this. The more you address problems early, the less likely they are to become bigger issues.

Sharing Your Self-Expectations

I wanted to make sure that I added this part to remind us all that we are human, and that the best connection we ever have is that of humanness. Sharing our dreams and expectations that we put upon ourselves with others, especially our employees, and communicating with them in a very authentic way allows them to understand "why" we are doing what we are doing. It offers them a chance to see some of our motivation and passion that will help the company and everyone else succeed. As you become more comfortable with sharing your self-expectations, you become more transparent and authentic. That is when the true power comes, the power that will lead to a level of buy-in that you've never seen before.

Getting the Good On Board

Getting the "good" on board—that is, good employees who align with your organization's values—is critical to creating an environment conducive to achieving your goals and vision. Because getting the "bad" out is often accomplished by outnumbering them by the good, we will focus on using your values as a filter to ensure that you are bringing in the right people, putting them in appropriate positions, and then pumping in the energy to support them so they buy in to all that supports your vision for the company.

Hire Based on Values

Each company has its own hiring process. Some are built on structures of intellectual testing, honesty testing, and drug testing, and, in the end, we try to determine who is the best fit. In this process, we all follow certain industry standards based on previous human resource experience. In what part of the process should you, as a leader, get involved? After an applicant has passed the necessary qualifications level of the job hiring process, it's time for you and your values to become part of the process.

Remember, we can teach skills; we can enhance knowledge; and we can provide experience. However, if the core values of the potential employee and the core values of the organization do not align, disaster lies ahead. There is a saying, "Hire slow, and fire fast." I get that process, but I want to enhance that by adding, "Follow your values, always." When your guts tell you somebody is not aligning with your values, you need to dismiss that person—or risk affecting the well-being of the entire company.

The hiring process is the gateway into your organization. We have borders to our country. We have borders to our states. We have fences around our military installations for protection. Why should we not protect our companies the same way? We should be absolutely vehement about standing guard at the gate of our companies. As a leader, you are responsible for taking this stand. You must ensure that the good people get in, and the bad stay out. This is an immense responsibility, but the peace and success of you and your company depends on it. Some will try to get by. Some may even be successful. But if you are strict about holding to your values and constantly work them, if you are hiring based on questions and qualifications surrounding them, and if you empower your employees to do the same, then you will likely prevail in hiring the right person for the job. And that is much more important than simply hiring the person with the right skill set.

The Great Like to Work with The Great

It is no surprise that if you are going to put a ton of energy, expertise, and skill into something, and you are expected to work with other people in a group, you want them to be just as committed, just as excellent as you intend to be. And if that turns out not to be the case, then it is no surprise that you would want to leave that group so you can find another one that meets your standards. Our companies are no different. If we allow subpar character into our companies, instead of flushing out the bad, we will lose the good because good employees have more options.

It is the negative, the unproductive, the unemployable who have nowhere to go, and those are the people who will stay if you let them. That is why the hiring process is so critical. You need to reward your great employees with other great employees. Set a standard. Set a high standard, not only based on results, but based on expected character and actions. These standards, once understood among all employees, will become the status quo. Positive peer pressure will emerge, as everyone expects those characteristics or standards to be adhered to or met. When that happens, respect becomes the norm. This is a truly amazing time. This is what we all work to achieve.

When you encounter an organization where respect is the norm, you just know it. You walk in there, and you can feel it. These organizations attract strong stakeholders, not just customers, not just vendors, but potential employees who hear that your company is a great place to work, that it's a place where they will be treated well. In the end, that is what great employees are seeking—a workplace that is encouraging and supportive, a place that will give them an opportunity to succeed and see their dreams materialize. By creating a positive environment, you will attract positive people. Unfortunately, on the flip side, the negative will do the same. Remember: You are the leader, and you are responsible for being the gatekeeper of your work environment.

CHAPTER 18:

Reward, Reward, Reward

Rewards are a great way to reinforce positive actions, and they do not have to be monetary. In this chapter, we will discuss how to reward employees, what to reward, and why the benefits, frequency, and the energy that you put into the reward matter. We will also examine the benefit of using multilayered rewards that encompass an individual as well as the group, highlighting the fact that individual success is not possible without group support.

A Little Goes a Long Way

In the reward process, it is always tough to know exactly what motivates individual people and really makes them appreciative of their reward. We don't want to give them something that they dismiss or don't appreciate, but unfortunately it's sometimes difficult to understand what makes different people tick. We might end up limiting our rewards to one large, big awards day that happens once a year. Again, it's important to remember that such a practice fails to reward the everyday contributions of employees who help build the success of the "stars" and the company's overall success. For example, in an organization of 200, 199 will not get the grand prize or award. That's why I suggest just the opposite practice. I suggest cards, knickknacks, a free lunch, something simple but given out frequently and with thought.

We all respond to positive reinforcements when we do the right thing—they guide us as we continue moving along the path. You can think of positive reinforcements or rewards like a GPS. If these devices simply told us when we have reached our destination, they would not be helpful. It's in their informing us when a turn is coming up, so we can be prepared and know that we're going in the right direction, that they have real value. Our employees are no different, and the positive little rewards are very possibly much more important to them than the big ones.

The Power of Personal

The frequency of rewards is important, but personalization is what really makes an impact. Think about it: If you get a letter in the mail that says, "Congratulations, you win," the first thing you think is "Everybody got this—it's a form letter." On the other hand, when you receive a personal note acknowledging precisely what you did and why you're being recognized, that has staying power because it's individualized and it tells us that we really must matter, and that we indeed are moving in the right direction.

Not only is the personalization of the delivery important, but so is the effort with which it's given. We do not want to have a weekly meeting where we simply call out names, hand out the latest prizes, and then send people back to work. Make it exciting (unless, of course, you are confident that the person receiving the award truly abhors public recognition). I don't care if you have to hire a mariachi band or a singing telegram. Make it exciting so the employee anticipates what's coming, is excited when it does, and always remembers the occasion.

Reward the Core

When we are trying to decide what we should base rewards to our employees on, there is really only one area to reward consistently—values. That which is most important is what should be rewarded. Remember, without our values, our companies have no core. If we have no core, we will wither away and become history like so many other organizations before us. The core of what we are is our values.

As our values are rewarded, people will look for ways to enhance them. As they enhance our values, they enhance our company. As they enhance our company, we are able to enhance their lives. As we are able to enhance their lives, they want to enhance our company by enhancing the values. See the connection? That is the power of doing something simple over and over again for the right reasons and getting amazing results. It is the circle of success.

Reward the Little; the Big Have Their Own

In many of our companies, we automatically recognize the salesperson with the most sales or the person who has produced the most widgets, but those people are probably also the highest compensated in our organizations, and that is a reward in itself. I suggest rewarding the little things that other employees do every day, making sure our supervisors and co-workers stay focused on the details that add up to make the big successes possible.

An example in a sales environment would be that instead of just celebrating when we win the big account, we should also celebrate somebody going out every day making, let's say, twenty calls, if that is the goal—because without those twenty calls day in and day out, and working hard, the closing of the big account would have never transpire. Focusing on the everyday tasks that make the big accomplishments possible reminds your team that success comes from doing the little things, and not just hoping for the big things to happen.

Part 4: Practice Your Peace

CHAPTER 19:

Greatness Happens Every Day

Many think of greatness as the goal at the end of a journey, having finally reached the mountain's summit. From my experience, I believe greatness is actually embedded within the bricks that make up the path.

We Are Our Habits

As I described in chapter 1, in late 2014, I had the opportunity to climb Mount Kilimanjaro in Africa. It is the largest freestanding mountain in the world, and the summit is 19,341 feet above sea level. For someone like myself who is—or at least was—not a hiker, not a climber, and not really even much of an outdoors person, this was an epic challenge. After all I grew up on the flatlands of North Dakota. When I tell people about this, the first thing they typically ask is, "Wow, what was the view from the top like?" I give the response you would expect: "It was amazing. You could see for hundreds of miles. You could actually see Kenya all the way from Tanzania, because we were so high. It was an amazing view to say the least."

Although the view was fantastic, if people see that summit as the true greatness, they missed the thousands of steps I had to take on the way to the top. When you talk about the journey in a general state, then yeah, the goal tends to be what you see as the greatness within the journey. But when you examine the details, you begin to see the amazing greatness that lies within all of the smaller steps. For example, on the first day of our six-day climb, I was walking, and the guide pointed out some birds that were up in the tree. I looked up and saw the birds' amazing wingspans. Entranced, I watched them while still walking. Taking a step down, I rolled my ankle and collapsed to the trail floor. I quickly got up; shook off the little bit of embarrassment from falling, and began to realize that my ankle was getting pretty sore.

When we arrived at camp for the night, I knew that I had to ignore the pain and just hope that it didn't swell too much. Fortunately, it did not, but it was sore, and it reminded me every step during that next day that I had to keep pushing. On the third day, we reached the Horombo Huts, and altitude sickness relieved me of my appetite. I wasn't feeling well at all. I just didn't eat, and I was struggling. Because I didn't eat, I became a little weaker and a little more fatigued. I had to force myself to consume some food so I could maintain my energy level. I also had to increase my liquid intake so I wouldn't get dehydrated at the higher elevations.

At the time it is happening, we do not see our individual steps as greatness. Sometimes they are monotonous, sometimes even filled with drudgery. But if we consciously examine how we arrived at our destination, we can see how defining and critical each step really was. When I looked back on my journey up Mount Kilimanjaro, I could see that had I not forced myself through that injury and challenge, I never would have made it to the top. On the day of the final ascent, we actually started at midnight. Because I could not sleep the day before, I woke up already tired, even slightly exhausted. We were already at thinner altitudes, so that stressed my body even more. As we left the final Kibo Hut, the base camp for the final ascent, I was exhausted.

Every step felt like I was wearing concrete boots: one more step, one more step, one more step. As I was going through that, I recognized that I had to intentionally push through this to reach my goal, but I also saw that I needed to press through this because it was the challenge at hand. It was what I was being called to do right then and there. I think that is where sometimes we lose focus. We focus on our ultimate goals so strongly that we forget that the challenge is right there in front of us.

When looking at greatness, try to remember that it is in the everyday. It's not found in the banners, trophies, or the awards. That is merely where we are recognized for the greatness we have achieved. Our greatness is defined, created, actualized every day. That day when you wake up and it's tough to get out of bed, but you force yourself to do so because you know you must get to work, get to school, get to a workout—that is greatness. Those small acts do not result in a lot of fanfare, but without that, you never earn the promotion; you never get the scholarship; you never achieve the desired workout results and the flat abs. You don't get the results if you don't put the effort in every day.

CHAPTER 20:

So Simple, So Hard

So there it is: the secrets to being able to lead from a place of peace. When you look at the lessons in this book, I am guessing you probably said, "Yeah, that makes sense" to most of the ideas discussed here and that, too, makes sense. It is the implementation that holds all the juice. In these pages, I have shared a simplified way for using your values, principles, and faith to become the leader—and the person—you seek to be. Indeed, intentionally trying to Do Right, Be Right, and Pay It Forward in all your interactions and decisions provides a road map to a successful future for you and your company, a future that you can feel proud of.

The challenge is that the road map takes you through a front-loaded rough terrain of discipline and that is where we most often lose our steam, lose our way. But if you commit yourself to fighting through that, it becomes easier with time. Trust me!

Most of the lessons in this book came through my own personal trials and self-exploration. At one time, I was a driven leader who respected only results. I made many mistakes, failed many times, and did things I regret. I had to learn from the errors of my ways. Fortunately, I did. Bit by bit, I discovered that this was not the way I wanted to be. And I learned that if I was going to change and create real peace in my life—the peace that comes from living by my values and principles—it was not going to come through some potion, and I could not buy the results. Change would only come by putting in the hard, consistent work.

The simple key to being successful is taking all of these processes and creating a thoughtful, intentional road map authored by yourself that implements small pieces, and then builds on your successes. PLEASE note: You do not need to have this all implemented next week. This is not just another project, but rather a way of living—something you work on today and every day for the rest of your life.

My truest hope is that the tips and processes in this book help you find the peace and contentment in your life that we all long for. When we define, and go about our lives in a way that creates value for the world, that is the epitome of success!

As discussed in the introduction, while I hope that all of the ideas in this book resonate with you and bring you value, my desire is that you would begin by taking one idea and integrating it deep within the habitual part of your life where you live it every day. Taking any one of the concepts to that level is not a tomorrow accomplishment, even though you can begin it that soon and that easily. It is a process that takes time and repetition. To become second nature, it will need to be tested against the full distraction of a busy life, and all the other options vying for your attention.

That's the rub. Anyone can say that they agree with these concepts for intentional living, and anyone can do this for a week or two, but something quite amazing happens if you do even just one thing over and over again. It grows and takes on a life of its own, and the momentum makes the next commitment easier. For me, it all started with the practice of beginning each day by stating three things I was grateful for, and then thinking about those things for five minutes. From there, making positive actions became easier, and living with intention became a habit; from there, the challenges of business and life fell into proper perspective.

May your journey be just as peaceful and rewarding!

www.ingramcontent.com/pod-product-compliance
Lightning Source LLC
Chambersburg PA
CBHW070257190526
45169CB00001B/448